AN ADAPTED CLASSIC

Silas Marner

George Eliot

GLOBE FEARON
EDUCATIONAL PUBLISHER

A Division of Simon & Schuster
Upper Saddle River, New Jersey

Adapter: Tony Napoli
Project Editor: Kristen Shepos-Salvatore
Editorial Supervisor: Sandra Widener
Editorial Assistant: Kathleen Kennedy
Production Editor: Alan Dalgleish
Marketing Manager: Sandra Hutchison
Art Supervision: Patricia Smythe
Electronic Page Production: Luc VanMeerbeek
Cover and Interior Illustrator: Charlie Shaw

Printed in the United States of America.
1 2 3 4 5 6 7 8 9 10 99 98 97 96

ISBN: 0-835-91887-4

GLOBE FEARON EDUCATIONAL PUBLISHER
A Division of Simon & Schuster
Upper Saddle River, New Jersey

CONTENTS

ABOUT THE AUTHOR

George Eliot was the name used by English writer Mary Anne Evans. Evans was born in Warwickshire, England, in 1819. Her father, an estate manager, was very religious. He sent Mary Anne and her sister away to boarding schools. While there, they became very religious as well. Mary Anne's devotion to religion would stay with her during her youth.

After the death of her mother and the marriage of her sister, Mary Anne took charge of her father's house. As she grew older, her religious views changed. Her faith in Christianity became weaker. She decided she could no longer go to church in good faith. This caused a deep conflict with her father. After briefly living away from him, she agreed to return to her father's house and go back to church. However, she was against formal religion for the rest of her life.

After her father's death in 1849, Mary Anne moved to London. She became assistant editor of the *Westminster Review*. The *Review* was one of the top literary and political journals of that time. In London, she met George Henry Lewes, a drama critic, actor, and author. He and Evans fell in love. Lewes was married, but his wife had left him. Because of the laws at the time, there was no chance that he would be able to get a legal divorce. Starting in 1854, Lewes and Evans lived together as husband and wife until his death. This action, which was shocking for the time, made them outcasts at first. When their commitment to each other became clear, though, they were accepted by their friends and society as a married couple.

George Eliot's career as a fiction writer began in 1857. She published three short stories in *Blackwood's Magazine*. Her first novel, *Adam Bede,* was published in

1859. It was an instant success. Her other novels include *The Mill on the Floss* (1860), *Silas Marner* (1861), and *Romola* (1862-63). *Middlemarch*(1866), which many think is her best book, was published in parts throughout 1871 and 1872.

After George Lewes died in 1878, Eliot married an old friend, an American banker named J.W. Cross. Soon after, on December 22, 1880, she died.

ADAPTER'S NOTE

In preparing this edition of *Silas Marner*, we have kept closely to what George Eliot wrote. We have modified some vocabulary and shortened and simplified many sentences and paragraphs. None of the story, however, has been omitted.

PREFACE

Silas Marner is the story of a 19th century English weaver. His life is changed forever when he adopts and raises an orphaned two-year-old girl.

Silas Marner makes use of George Eliot's childhood memories. The idea for *Silas Marner* came from her memory of seeing a linen-weaver with a bag on his back. The novel uses other memories of her childhood, including her wide knowledge of the different forms of Christianity.

In her writings about her works, Eliot stated that the idea of God is based on human goodness. In *Silas Marner*, as in her other works, Eliot is concerned with people's dealings with each other for good and ill. She said that she wanted the book to show how "pure, natural human relations" could redeem people's lives.

CHARACTERS

SILAS MARNER
>A weaver

EPPIE
>Silas's adopted daughter

GODFREY CASS
>Yhe wealthy Squire Cass's eldest son

NANCY LAMMETER
>A wealthy landowner's daughter

DUNSTAN CASS
>One of Godfrey's brothers

SQUIRE CASS
>Raveloe's most important citizen, and the father of Godfrey and Dunstan

PRISCILLA LAMMETER
>Nancy's sister

MR. LAMMETER
>Father of Nancy and Priscilla

MOLLY FARREN
>Godfrey's wife

DOLLY WINTHROP
>A kindly Raveloe woman

AARON WINTHROP
>Dolly's son

BEN WINTHROP
>Dolly's husband

MR. MACEY
>A tailor in Raveloe

MR. SNELL
>The landlord of the Rainbow Inn

MR. CRACKENTHORP
>Rector of the church in Raveloe

DR. KIMBLE
>A pharmacist in Raveloe

Chapter 1

There once was a time when the spinning wheels hummed busily in the farmhouses. And in those days, certain pale, small men could be seen wandering the countryside. These men looked like the last survivors of a lost race.

The shepherd's dog barked fiercely when one of these strange-looking men appeared. For what dog likes a figure bent under a heavy bag? And these men rarely walked about without carrying such a bag. The shepherd himself, though, knew that the bag held nothing but thread or linen. Still, he wasn't sure that this trade of weaving could be carried on without some help from the Evil One.

In that far-off time, superstition surrounded every unusual person or thing. Even the visits of the peddler or knife-grinder[1] were looked upon with suspicion. No one knew where wandering men had their homes or where they came from. And how was a man to be explained unless someone knew his father and his mother? Those scattered linen weavers were always thought of as strange by their village neighbors. These weavers usually acquired the odd habits that belong to those who are always lonely.

In the early years of this century, there was such a linen weaver, named Silas Marner. He worked in a stone cottage near the village of Raveloe. His cottage stood among a row of shrub trees near the edge of a deserted stone pit. The local boys of Raveloe lived in fear of Marner. Many of them were fascinated by the

---

1. **peddler or knife-grinder** traveling salesmen

movement of Silas's loom.[2] They would sometimes peep through the window of his cottage.

Marner was not pleased by these acts. He would open his door and fix on them a gaze that would make them flee in terror. They had perhaps heard stories about him from their mothers and fathers. There were rumors that Silas Marner could cure folks' illnesses, if he had a mind to. There was even talk that, if you could speak the devil[3] fair enough, he might save you the cost of a doctor. Talk about demon worship could still be heard in some places at that time among the older peasants. Raveloe was such a place.

It lay in the rich central plain of what we call Merry England. It was set in a snug, wooded hollow, a good hour's journey by horseback from the nearest turnpike.[4] The sound of public opinion never reached there. Still, it was an important-looking village. It had a fine, old church and large churchyard in the heart of it. The surrounding farms were very successful.

It was 15 years since Silas Marner had first come to Raveloe. His plain appearance would have meant nothing to people of average culture and experience. But to these villagers, he was strange. This was because of the nature of his work. It was also because he had come to Raveloe from points "north'ard."

Silas had his way of life. He never invited anyone inside his cottage. He never strolled into the village to drink a pint at the Rainbow Inn. He sought no man or woman except for one of two reasons. One reason was for his work. The other was to get basic things to live on.

This view that Marner was strange came from the

---

2. **loom** machine for weaving thread into cloth
3. **speak the devil** praise the devil
4. **turnpike** main road

story that Jem Rodney told. He said that one night, as he was returning home, he saw Marner leaning against a post with a heavy bag on his back. When he approached Marner, he saw that his eyes were set like a dead man's. Jem spoke to him and shook him. Marner's limbs were stiff. And he held the bag as if his hands had been made of iron.

Jem had just made up his mind that the weaver was dead. Then Marner came all right again, said, "Good night," and walked off. Some said Marner must have been in a "fit." It was a word used to describe things that could not be explained. Others thought this fit helped explain how Marner was able to cure Sally Oates. Sally's heart had been beating enough to burst her body. For two months she had been under a doctor's care, with no help. Yet Silas, who knew herbs, had gotten her to sleep like a baby. It was said he might cure more folks if he would. It was worth speaking well of him, if only to keep him from doing you harm.

Silas Marner's life before he'd come to Raveloe had a history. He'd belonged to a narrow religious sect.[5] He had been thought of in the assembled church of Lantern Yard as a good man of strong faith. At one prayer meeting, he had fallen into the state in which Jem Rodney once found him. It lasted for more than an hour, and was looked upon as a special gift with religious importance.

Silas had been close friends with another member of the church, named William Dane. He too, was thought to be a good, faithful man. Silas did not suspect that his friendship with Dane would suffer when Silas became engaged to a young servant woman

---

5. **religious sect** religious group that follows a set of extreme beliefs

named Sarah. It was a great delight to him when William was present during Silas's and Sarah's Sunday visits.

It was at this time that Silas's prayer meeting fit took place. William's view jarred with the general sympathy toward Silas. William observed that this trance looked more like a visit from Satan than proof of a divine gift. Silas felt no anger, only pain, at his friend's view.

Soon after, the church deacon became very ill. He was looked after night and day by members of the church. Silas and William often took turns at night watching him. One would relieve the other at two in the morning.

One night, while Silas was beside him, the old man seemed to stop breathing. Silas examined him, and became convinced the man was dead. It was already four in the morning, and Silas was surprised that William had not appeared.

Silas went quickly to get help and then went home. Later that morning, William and the minister came to summon him to Lantern Yard. When Silas arrived, he learned that a sum of money had been stolen from the deacon's bureau. The minister had found Silas's knife inside the drawer where the money had been. He was told not to hide his sin, but to confess and ask forgiveness.

Silas was shocked. Then he said, "God will clear me. I know nothing about the knife being there, or the money being gone. Search my home. You will find nothing more than a few pounds[6] of my own savings. William knows I have had this for six months."

The search was made. William Dane found the well-

---

6. pounds units of English money

known bag, empty, tucked behind Silas's chest of draw-ers. He begged his friend to confess and not hide his sin.

"William, you have known me for nine years," Silas said. "Have you ever known me to tell a lie?"

"How do I know what you may have done in your heart?" William said. "Satan may now have an advan-tage over you."

Silas was about to answer, when he suddenly flushed. "I remember now. The knife wasn't in my pocket."

"I know nothing of what you mean," William said.

Silas would give no further explanation. "I can say nothing," he said. "God will clear me."

The church members followed their way of learning the truth. They prayed and drew lots to determine Silas's guilt. Silas prayed as well. He prayed for divine help, for his trust in man had been cruelly bruised.

The lots declared that Silas Marner was guilty. As everyone rose to leave, Silas went to William. "I last used the knife to cut a strap for you. I don't remember putting it in my pocket again. You stole the money. And you have put the plot at my door."

William said, "I leave our brethren to judge whether this is the voice of Satan or not. I can only pray for you, Silas."

Marner went home. He sat alone in despair. He made no attempt to visit Sarah and tell her his story. The next day, he received a message from her. She con-sidered their engagement to be over. A month later, Sarah was married to William Dane. Not long after that, Silas left Lantern Yard for good.

Raveloe could not have been more unlike Silas Marner's native land of windswept hills. In his cottage, he felt hidden from the heavens by the large trees. There was nothing that seemed to have any relation to his life in Lantern Yard. The Divine Power in which he had trusted seemed very far away from this land to which he had come.

His first movement after the shock had been to work at his loom. He worked all the time. He worked far into the night to finish Mrs. Osgood's table linen sooner than she expected. He seemed to weave, like the spider, from pure impulse, without thinking.

At last Mrs. Osgood's table linen was finished. Silas was paid in gold. His earnings in his native town had been lower. He had been paid weekly, and a large part of his earnings had gone to his church and charity. Now, for the first time in his life, he had five bright guineas[7] put into his hand. No one expected a share of them. And he loved no one enough to offer anyone a share. The weaver's hand had known hard-earned money before. For 20 years, money had stood to him as the symbol of earthly good. He had seemed to love it little when every penny had its purpose for him. But now, when all purpose was gone, he still had the habit of looking at the money with a sense of fulfilled effort. Silas walked home with his money. He looked at it and thought it was brighter in the gathering gloom.

About this time, something happened that opened the possibility of fellowship with his neighbors. One day, Silas was taking a pair of shoes to be mended when he saw the cobbler's wife, Sally Oates, seated by the fire. She was suffering from heart disease. Silas recognized the symptoms as the same ones his mother

---

7. **guineas** English gold coins used from the late 17th to the early 19th centuries

had before she died.

Silas felt a rush of pity. He then recalled the relief his mother had found from a special herb. He promised to bring Sally Oates something to ease her pain.

For the first time since he'd come to Raveloe, Silas felt a link between his past and present life. It might have been the beginning of his rescue from the insect-like life into which he had shrunk. His medicine helped Sally Oates. This fact became quick news. It was one thing for a doctor to help cure a sick villager. It was quite another when a weaver, who came from "who knows where," did it. It was clear that Silas must have charms as well as "stuff."

Silas was soon beset by mothers who wanted him to help cure their babies' illnesses. Men who wanted stuff to cure pains also came to his cottage. To make sure that Silas said yes, the people brought their silver.

Silas could have made a profitable trade for himself, but doing this for money held no interest for him. One after another, he drove the people away. No one believed him when he said he knew no charms and could work no cures. People blamed him for any accident or new attack they had after he turned them down. His kind act toward Sally Oates gave him only a temporary sense of brotherhood. In the end, it only increased the dislike he and his neighbors felt for each other. And it made his isolation complete.

Gradually, the gold coins he earned grew to a heap. He tried to spend less and less on himself and still keep himself strong enough to work 16 hours a day.

He began to hoard his money. Marner wanted the heaps of ten to grow into a square, and then into a larger square. Every added guinea bred a desire for more. He handled his coins and counted them at night when his work was done. He drew them out to enjoy

their companionship. He had taken up some bricks in his floor underneath his loom. Here, he had placed his gold and silver coins in an iron pot. When he was done counting, he replaced the pot and covered the bricks with sand.

So, year after year, Silas Marner lived alone. His guineas rose in his iron pot. His life was reduced to weaving and hoarding. He had no thought of why he performed these acts.

Marner's face and figure shrank and bent in relation to the objects of his life. His large eyes, once trusting and dreamy, now looked as if they could only see very small things, like tiny grain. His eyes hunted for it everywhere. He was so withered, the children called him "Old Master Marner." He was not yet 40.

During the day, he sat at his loom. His ears filled with the same sounds. His eyes bent down close to the same slowly growing web of thread. At night came his happiness. He closed his shutters and locked his doors. Then he drew out his gold.

The heap of coins had long ago become too large for the iron pot. He had made two thick leather bags for them. He spread the coins out and bathed his hands in them. Then he counted them and set them in piles.

His thoughts were always on his loom and his money. This was true even when he made his way through the fields and the lanes to fetch and carry home more work. His steps never wandered in search of the once familiar herbs. They belonged to the past, a past from which his life had shrunk away.

This is the history of Silas Marner until 15 years after he came to Raveloe. But about Christmas of that 15th year, a second great change came over Marner's life. His life became mixed in an important way with the lives of his neighbors.

Chapter 2

The greatest man in Raveloe was Squire Cass. He lived in the large red house with the handsome flight of stone steps in front and the high stables behind it. The Squire's wife had died long ago. The Red House was without that presence of the wife and mother that is the fountain of wholesome love and fear in parlor[1] and kitchen. This helped to explain why the proud Squire spent his time in the parlor of the Rainbow Inn rather than in his own. It also helped to explain, perhaps, why his sons had turned out rather ill. Raveloe was not a place where moral criticism was harsh, but it was thought a weakness in the Squire that he had kept all his sons at home in idleness.

People shook their heads at the course of the second son, Dunstan, commonly called Dunsey Cass. His taste for gambling might turn out to be a sowing of something worse than wild oats. Dunsey was a spiteful fellow who seemed to enjoy his drink more when other people were sober. To be sure, the neighbors said, it was no matter what became of Dunsey, provided he didn't bring trouble on a family like Squire Cass's.

However, it would be a thousand pities if Mr. Godfrey, the eldest son, should take to the same road as his brother. Lately, he seemed to be doing just that. If he went on that way, he would lose Miss Nancy Lammeter. There was something wrong, that was quite clear. Mr. Godfrey didn't look half as fresh-colored and open as he used to.

At one time everyone was saying what a handsome

---

1. **parlor** living room or den

couple he and Miss Nancy Lammeter would make. If she could come to be mistress at the Red House there would be a fine change. But if Mr. Godfrey didn't turn over a new leaf, he might say good-bye to Miss Nancy Lammeter.

It was Godfrey who was standing with his back to the fire in the dark parlor one late November afternoon. This was in the 15th year of Silas Marner's life at Raveloe. Soon, the sound of a heavy step, along with a whistle, was heard across the entrance hall.

The door opened, and a thickset, heavy-looking young man entered. It was Dunsey. At the sight of him Godfrey's face changed from an expression of gloom to one of hatred.

"Well, Master Godfrey, what do you want with me?" Dunsey said in a mocking tone. "You're my elder and better, you know. I was obliged to come when you sent for me."

"Why, this is what I want," Godfrey said savagely. "I want to tell you, I must hand over that rent of Fowler's to the Squire. Or else I have to tell him I gave it to you. He's threatening to go to Fowler for it. It will all be out soon, whether I tell him or not. So, get the money, and pretty quickly, will you?"

"Oh!" said Dunsey with a sneer. He came nearer to his brother and looked in his face. "Suppose you get the money yourself, and save me the trouble, eh? Since you were so kind as to hand it over to me, you'll not refuse to pay it back for me. It was your brotherly love made you do it, you know."

Godfrey bit his lip and clenched his fist. "Don't come near me with that look, else I'll knock you down."

"Oh, no, you won't," said Dunsey, turning away on his heel, however. "Because I'm such a good-natured brother, you know. I might get you turned out of house

and home. I might tell the Squire how his handsome
son was married to that nice young woman, Molly
Farren. And how he was very unhappy because he
couldn't live with his drunken wife. Then I should slip
into your place as comfortable as could be. But you see,
I don't do it—I'm so easy and good-natured. You'll take
any trouble for me. You'll get the 100 pounds for me. I
know you will."

"How can I get the money?" said Godfrey, shaking.
"I haven't a shilling[2] to bless myself with. And it's a lie
that you'd slip into my place. You'd get yourself turned
out too, that's all. For if you begin telling tales, I'll follow. Bob's my father's favorite—you know that very
well. He'd only think himself well rid of you."

"Never mind," said Dunsey. "It would be very pleasant for me to go in your company. You're such a handsome brother, and we've always been so fond of
quarreling with one another. I shouldn't know what to
do without you. But you'd like better for us both to
stay at home together. I know you would. So you'll
manage to get that little sum of money. And I'll bid
you good-bye, though I'm sorry to part."

Dunstan was moving off, but Godfrey rushed after
him and grabbed him by the arm.

"I tell you I have no money," Godfrey said. "I can
get no money."

"Borrow from old Kimble," Dunsey said.

"I tell you, he won't lend me any more, and I won't
ask him."

"Well then, sell your horse—sell Wildfire."

"Yes, that's easy talking," Godfrey replied. "I must
have the money right away."

"Well, you've only got to ride him to the hunt tomor-

---

2. shilling   former unit of English money

row," Dunsey said. "Bryce and Keating will be there for sure. You'll get more bids than one."

"Yes, and get back home at eight o'clock, splashed up to the chin. I'm going to Mrs. Osgood's birthday dance."

"Oh ho!" said Dunsey. "And there's sweet Miss Nancy coming. And we shall dance with her and promise never to be naughty again, and be taken into favor—"

"Hold your tongue about Miss Nancy, you fool," Godfrey said, turning red. "Or else I'll throttle you."

"What for?" Dunsey replied. "You have a very good chance. It would be saving time if Molly should happen to take a drop too much laudanum[3] some day and make a widower of you. Miss Nancy wouldn't mind being a second if she didn't know it. And you've got a good-natured brother who will keep your secret well, because you'll be so very obliging to him."

"I'll tell you what it is," Godfrey said, shaking and pale again. "My patience is pretty near at an end. If you had a little more sharpness in you, you might know that you may urge a man a bit too far. I may as well tell the Squire everything myself. I should get you off my back, if I got nothing else. And, after all, he'll know sometime. Molly's been threatening to come herself and tell him about our marriage. So don't flatter yourself that your secrecy is worth any price you choose to ask. You drain me of money till I have nothing to give her, and she'll do as she threatens some day. I'll tell my father everything myself, and you may go to the devil."

Dunsey saw that he had overshot his mark. But he said, with unconcern, "As you please, but I'll have a

---

3. **laudanum** substance made of the drug Opium

drink of ale first."

"It's just like you," Godfrey burst out bitterly, "to talk about my selling Wildfire. He's the last thing I've got to call my own and the best bit of horseflesh I've ever had in my life. And if you had a spark of pride in you, you'd be ashamed to see the stables emptied. But it's my belief that you'd sell yourself, if it was only for the pleasure of making somebody feel he'd got a bad bargain."

"Ay, ay, you do me justice," Dunstan said, "for which reason I advise you to let me sell Wildfire. I'd ride him to the hunt tomorrow for you, with pleasure."

"You want me to trust my horse to you?"

"As you please," Dunstan said. "It's you who's got to pay Fowler's money. You received the money and you told the Squire it wasn't paid. You chose to be so obliging as to give it to me, that was all. If you don't want to pay the money, let it alone. But I was willing to help you by selling the horse, as it's not convenient for you to go so far tomorrow."

Godfrey was silent for some moments. His rage was finally mastered by his fear. Then he said, "Well, you mean no nonsense about the horse, eh? You'll sell him all fair and hand over the money? If you don't, you know, everything will go to smash, for I've got nothing else to trust to. And you'll have less pleasure in pulling the house over my head, when your own skull's to be broken, too."

"Ay, ay," Dunstan said, rising, "all right. I thought you'd come around. I'll get you 120 for him, if I get you a penny."

"And take care to keep sober tomorrow. Or else you'll get pinched on your head coming home, and Wildfire might be the worse for it."

"Make your tender heart easy," Dunstan said, opening the door. "You never knew me to see double when I've got a bargain to make. It would spoil all the fun."

With that, Dunstan slammed the door behind him. He left Godfrey to his bitter thinking about life in his six-and-twentieth year. For four years, he had thought of Nancy Lammeter. He wooed her with patient worship as the woman who made him think of the future with joy. She would be his wife and would make home lovely to him, as his father's home had never been.

Yet the hope of this paradise had not been enough to save him from a course that shut him out of it forever. He had let himself be dragged into mud and slime, in which it was useless to struggle. Still, there was one position worse than the present: when the ugly secret was out. Then Godfrey would have to face his father, and know he was banished from the sight of Nancy Lammeter. The good-hearted Godfrey Cass was fast becoming a bitter man.

What was he to do this evening to pass the time? He might as well go to the Rainbow Inn and hear all about the cockfighting. Everybody was there, and what else was there to be done?

Dunstan Cass set off in the raw morning for the hunt. He went along the lane that passed by the ground called the Stone Pit. Nearby stood the cottage where Silas Marner had lived for 15 years. The spot looked very dreary at this season. That was Dunstan's first thought as he came close. The second was that the old fool of a weaver had a great deal of money hidden somewhere. How was it that he had never thought of suggesting to Godfrey that he should frighten or persuade the old fellow into lending him the money?

Dunstan almost turned the horse's head toward home again. Godfrey would be ready enough to accept the suggestion. He would grab eagerly at a plan that might save him from selling Wildfire. Still, Dunstan decided to go on. He preferred that Master Godfrey should be troubled. Besides, Dunstan enjoyed having a horse to sell, the chance to drive a bargain, and possibly take somebody in. So he rode on.

Bryce and Keating were there, as Dunstan was quite sure they would be.

"Heyday!" said Bryce, who had long had his eye on Wildfire. "You're on your brother's horse today. How's that?"

"Oh, I've swapped with him," Dunstan said, knowing his listener would not believe him. "Wildfire's mine now."

"What! Has he swapped with you for that big-boned hack of yours?" Bryce said. He was quite aware that he should get another lie in answer.

"Oh, there was a little account between us, and Wildfire made it even. I shall keep Wildfire now that I've got him. I got a bid of 150 for him the other day."

Bryce knew that Dunstan wanted to sell Wildfire, and Dunstan knew that Bryce knew it. Keating rode up now, and the process became more involved. It ended in the purchase of the horse by Bryce for 120. It was to be paid on the delivery of Wildfire, safe and sound, at the Batherly stables. It did occur to Dunsey that it might be wise to give up the day's hunting and go at once to Batherly.

However, he felt like a run, especially with a fine horse under him. Dunstan took one fence too many, though. He escaped without injury, but poor Wildfire turned on his leg and painfully panted his last breath.

He did not much mind about taking the bad news to Godfrey, for he had to offer him at the same time the idea of Marner's money. He decided to head back to

Raveloe right away.

It was now nearly four o'clock, and a mist was gathering. The sooner he got into the road the better. By the time he had reached the well-known Raveloe lanes, the mist had deepened and the evening darkness was upon him. He found the Stone Pits in an unexpected way—namely, by gleams of light that he guessed were coming from Silas Marner's cottage. That cottage and the money hidden within it had been in his mind continually during his walk. He had been imagining ways of tempting the weaver to part with his money in return for interest.

By the time he saw the light gleaming from Marner's cottage, it seemed a natural thing to strike up a dialogue with the weaver. He had other reasons as well. The weaver possibly had a lantern, and it was getting difficult for Dunstan to make his way along the lanes. The mist was passing into rain, and the lane was becoming very slippery.

When he arrived at the door, he knocked loudly, enjoying the idea that the old fellow would be frightened at the sudden noise. He heard no movement in reply. All was silent in the cottage. Dunstan knocked more loudly. Then without waiting for a reply, he pushed his fingers through the latch hole, hoping to shake the door.

To his surprise, at this motion, the door opened. He found himself in front of a bright fire that lit up every corner of the cottage. He saw the bed, the loom, the three chairs, and the table. But Marner was not there.

Where could he be at this time, on such an evening, with his door unlocked? Perhaps he had gone outside to bring in some fuel, or for some other brief purpose, and had fallen in the Stone Pit. That was an interesting idea to Dunstan. If the weaver was dead, who had a right to his money? Who would know where his money was hidden? Who would know that anybody had come to take it away?

The question, "Where is the money?" took possession of him. It made him quite forget that the weaver's death was not a certainty. There were only three hiding places where he had ever heard of cottagers' hoards being found: the thatch,[4] the bed, and a hole in the floor. Marner's cottage had no thatch. Dunstan was about to go to the bed when his eyes traveled over the floor. He noticed that in one place the sand over the bricks showed the marks of fingers. They had been careful to spread the sand over a certain place.

In an instant, Dunstan darted to that spot. He swept away the sand and discovered two loose bricks underneath. He lifted up the bricks and found the object of his search. For what could there be but money in those two leather bags? Dunstan felt round the hole, to be certain that it held no more. Then he quickly replaced the bricks and spread the sand over them.

Hardly more than five minutes had passed since he entered the cottage. But it seemed to Dunstan like a long while. He rose to his feet with the bags in his hand. He would hasten out into the darkness and then consider what he should do with the bags.

He closed the door behind him, that he might shut in the stream of light. A few steps would be enough to carry him beyond the gleams from the latch hole. The rain and darkness had gotten thicker and he was glad of it. It was awkward walking with both hands filled. When he had gone a yard or two, he might take his time. So, he stepped forward into the darkness.

---

4. **thatch** roof made of straw

Chapter 3

When Dunstan Cass turned his back on the cottage, Silas Marner was not more than 100 yards away from it. He was plodding along from the village with a coat thrown round his shoulders and with a lantern in his hand. His legs were weary, but his mind was at ease. Silas was thinking of his supper with pleasure. First, because it would be hot and tasty. And second, because it would cost him nothing. The little bit of pork was a present from that excellent housewife, Miss Priscilla Lammeter. Silas had, on this day, carried home to her a handsome piece of linen.

Supper was his favorite meal. It came at his time of happiness, when his heart warmed over his gold. Whenever he had roast meat, he had it for supper. This evening, he knotted his string around his bit of pork and twisted the string over his door key. Then he passed it through the kettle handle and attached it to the hanger to roast. It was only then that he remembered that he needed a piece of very fine twine to start a new piece of work in his loom early in the morning.

To lose time by going on errands in the morning was out of the question. It was a nasty fog to turn out into, but there were things that Silas loved better than his own comfort. So, he armed himself with his lantern and his old sack. And he set out on what, in ordinary weather, would have been a 20-minute errand. He could not have locked his door without undoing his well-knotted string and delaying his supper. It was not worth his while to do that.

He reached his door, pleased that his errand was done. He opened it, and to his shortsighted eyes everything was as he left it. He walked about the floor, putting aside his lantern, hat, and sack. So he merged the marks of Dunstan's feet on the sand in the marks of his own nailed boots. He moved his pork nearer to the fire. Then he sat down to the pleasure of tending the meat and warming himself at the same time.

Soon, he began to think it would be a long while to wait till after supper before he drew out his guineas. He felt it would be pleasant to see them on the table before him as he ate his feast. He rose and placed his candle on the floor near his loom. He swept away the sand and removed the bricks. The sight of the empty hole made his heart leap. But the belief that his gold was gone could not come at once. He felt only terror and the eager effort to put an end to the terror. He passed his trembling hand all about the hole, trying to think it possible that his eyes had deceived him. Then he held the candle in the hole and examined it closely, trembling more and more.

At last he shook so violently that he let the candle fall. He lifted his hands to his head, trying to steady himself, that he might think. Had he put his gold somewhere else last night and then forgotten it? He searched in every corner. He turned his bed over and shook it. He looked in his brick oven where he laid his sticks. When there was no other place to be searched, he kneeled down again and felt once more all around the hole. There was no untried place left for a moment's shelter from the terrible truth.

Silas got up from his knees, trembling. He put his hands to his head, and gave a wild ringing scream. For a few moments after, he stood still. But the cry had relieved him from the first maddening pressure of the truth. He turned and tottered toward his loom. He got into the seat where he worked, seeking this as the strongest proof of reality.

Now all false hopes had vanished, and the first shock of certainty was past. The idea of a thief began to present itself, and he entertained it eagerly. A thief might be caught and made to restore the gold. The thought brought some new strength with it. He started from his loom to the door. As he opened it the rain beat in upon him, for it was falling more and heavily. There were no footsteps to be tracked on such a night.

When had the thief come? During Silas's absence in the daytime the door had been locked. And there had been no marks of anyone having entered when he returned by daylight. In the evening, too, everything was the same as when he had left it. The sand and bricks looked as if they had not been moved. Was it a thief who had taken the bags? Or was it a cruel power that no hands could reach, which had delighted in making him a second time empty and alone? He shrank from this awful feeling, and fixed his mind on the robber with hands.

He thought about all the neighbors who had made any remarks or asked questions that might be suspicious. There was Jem Rodney, a known poacher.[1] He had often met Marner in his journeys across the fields. He had said something funny about the weaver's money. He had also once annoyed Marner by staying too long at his fire when he called to light his pipe. Jem Rodney was the man—there was ease in the thought. Jem could be found and made to restore the money.

Marner felt that he must go and proclaim his loss. And the great people in the village—the clergyman,

---

1. **poacher** someone who trespasses on land or hunts animals illegally

the constable,[2] and Squire Cass—would make Jem Rodney, or somebody else, deliver up the stolen money. He rushed out in the rain, under the feeling of this hope. He didn't care to lock his door. He felt as if he had nothing left to lose. He ran swiftly until he was nearly out of breath. Then he eased his pace as he entered the village to the Rainbow Inn. It was the place where Silas felt he was likely to find the powerful and important people of Raveloe. And it was where he could most quickly make his loss public.

The conversation at the Rainbow was in a high state of excitement when Silas approached the door of the inn. For the last few moments, there had been an argument and a discussion about ghosts.

"But I'm afraid of neither man nor ghost," said Mr. Dowlas, the farrier.[3] "And I'm ready to lay a fair bet..."

"There's folks, in my opinion, they can't see ghosts, not if they stood as plain as a fence post before them," said Mr. Snell, the landlord.[4]

"If ghosts want me to believe in them, let them stop hiding in the dark and in lonely places," Mr. Dowlas said. "Let them come where there's company and candles."

"As if ghosts would want to be believed in by anybody so ignorant," said Mr. Macey, a tailor and the parish clerk. He was disgusted with the farrier's failure to understand ghostly behavior.

Yet the next moment there seemed to be some evidence that ghosts might follow Dowlas's demand to come out in the open. For the pale thin figure of Silas

---

2. constable   a policeman of a town in England
3. farrier   someone who attends to or makes shoes for horses
4. landlord   innkeeper

Marner was suddenly seen standing in the warm light. He uttered no word, but looked around at the company with his strange, unearthly eyes. Every man present had the impression that he saw, not Silas Marner, but a ghost. The door by which Silas had entered was hidden by some seats. No one had noticed his approach.

Mr. Macey might be expected to feel some sort of triumph. Had he not always said that when Silas Marner was in that strange trance of his, his soul went loose from his body? Here was the proof. Nevertheless, on the whole, he would have been just as pleased without it.

For a few moments there was a dead silence. The landlord at last took on himself the task of addressing the ghost.

"Master Marner," he said agreeably, "what's your business here?"

"Robber!" said Silas, gasping. "I've been robbed! I want the constable and the justice and Squire Cass and Mr. Crackenthorp."

"Lay hold of him, Jem Rodney," said the landlord, the idea of a ghost passing. "He's off his head. He's wet through."

Jem Rodney sat near Marner's standing place, but he declined to help.

"Come and lay hold of him yourself, Mr. Snell, if you've a mind," said Jem. "He's been robbed and murdered too, for what I know," he added in a muttering tone.

"Jem Rodney!" said Silas, turning and fixing his strange eyes on the suspected man.

"Ay, Master Marner, what do you want with me?" Jem said. He was trembling a little and grabbed his can of ale as a defensive weapon.

"If it was you stole my money," Silas said, raising

his voice to a cry, "give it back. I won't meddle with you. I won't set the constable on you. Give it me back, and I'll let you—I'll let you have a guinea."

"Me stole your money!" said Jem angrily. "I'll pitch this can at your eye if you talk of my stealing your money."

"Come, come, Master Marner," said the landlord, now rising. He seized Marner by the shoulder. "If you've got any information, speak it out sensibly. And show us you're in your right mind, if you expect anybody to listen to you. You're as wet as a drowned rat. Sit down and dry yourself and speak straight."

"Ay, ay, make him sit down," said several voices at once. They were well pleased that the reality of ghosts remained an open question.

The landlord forced Marner to take off his coat and then to sit down on a chair apart from everyone else. The fears of the company were now forgotten in their curiosity. All faces were turned toward Silas. The landlord seated himself again and then spoke.

"Now then, Master Marner, what's this you've got to say? You've been robbed? Speak out."

Silas now told his story under much questioning. The mysterious character of the robbery became evident. The slight suspicion with which his hearers at first listened to him melted away. It was impossible for the neighbors to doubt that Marner was telling the truth. As Mr. Macey said, "Folks as had the devil to back 'em were not likely to be so mushed," as poor Silas was.

The neighbors were struck by a few strange facts. The robber had left no traces. He happened to know just when Silas would go away from home without locking his door. These things could not be known by any human. So this ill turn had been done to Marner by someone it was quite useless to set the constable after. Why this preternatural robber should wait until the door was unlocked was a question that did not present itself.

"It isn't Jem Rodney who has done this work, Master Marner," said the landlord. "Jem's been sitting here drinking like the most decent man in the parish. He's been here since before you left your house, by your own account."

"Ay, ay," said Mr. Macey. "Let's have no accusing of the innocent. That isn't the law. There must be folks to swear against a man before he can be taken up."

With a movement as new to him as anything within the last hour, Silas went close up to Jem. It was as if he wanted to assure himself of the expression on his face.

"I was wrong," Silas said. "There's nothing to witness against you, Jem. Only you'd been into my house more often than anybody else, and so you came into my head. I won't accuse, I won't accuse anybody, only—" Here, he lifted up his hands to his head and turned away in misery. "Only, I try—I try to think where my money can be."

"How much money might there be in the bags," Master Marner?" said Dowlas.

"Two hundred and seventy-two pounds, twelve and six pence, last night when I counted it," Silas said with a groan.

"Pooh! Why, they'd be none so heavy to carry. Some tramp's been in, that's all. And as for the no footmarks, and the bricks and the sand being all right—why, your eyes are pretty much like an insect's, Master Marner. You look so close, you can't see much at a time. It's my opinion, if I had been you, you wouldn't have thought you'd found everything as you left it.

"What I vote is, two people here should go with you to Master Kench, the constable," the farmer continued. "He's ill in bed. Get him to appoint one of us as his deputy. And then, if it's me as his deputy, I'll go back with you, Master Marner, and examine your premises."

Then, to the farrier's disgust, Mr. Macey objected to him proposing himself as a deputy constable. There was a hot debate upon this. And why, asked Mr. Macey, was Mr. Dowlas so eager to act in that capacity?

"I don't want to act as the constable," said the farrier. "And if there's some other man wants to go to Kench's in the rain, then let them go as they like it. You won't get me to go, I can tell you."

The landlord settled the dispute. Mr. Dowlas and Mr. Macey would both go. And so Silas, furnished with some old coverings, turned out with his two companions into the rain. He thought of the long night hours before him. He thought, not as those do who want to rest, but as those who expect to watch for the morning.

Chapter 4

Godfrey Cass returned home from Mrs. Osgood's party at midnight. He was not very surprised to learn that Dunsey had not come home. Perhaps he had not sold Wildfire and was waiting for another chance. Or perhaps, on that foggy afternoon, he had decided to spend the night at an inn at Batherley. Godfrey's mind was very full of Nancy Lammeter's looks and behavior, which the sight of her always produced in him. He didn't give much thought to Wildfire or to Dunstan's conduct.

The next morning, the whole village was excited by the story of the robbery. Godfrey, like everyone else, was busy gathering and discussing news about it and in visiting the Stone Pits. The rain had washed away all possibility of footmarks. But a close investigation of the spot had shown a tinderbox,[1] with flint and steel, half stuck in the mud. It was not Silas's tinderbox. The only one he had was still standing on his shelf. And the generally accepted feeling was that the tinderbox was connected to the robbery.

A few shook their heads. Their opinion was that it was not a robbery to have much light thrown on it by tinderboxes. Master Marner's tale had a queer look to it. Such things had been known as a man doing himself a mischief, and then setting the law to look for the do-er. When questioned as to what Master Marner had to gain by such a false story, they merely shook their

---

1. **tinderbox** metal box used for holding tinder (a substance that can be used to start a fire) and a flint and steel for striking a spark

heads. They said there was no knowing what some folks counted as gain. Besides, everybody had a right to their own opinions, grounds or no grounds. And the weaver, as everybody knew, was partly crazy.

These discussions were going on among the group outside the Rainbow. At the same time, a higher discussion was being carried on within. It took place under the guidance of Mr. Crackenthorp, the rector.[2] He was assisted by Squire Cass and other important members of the church.

Mr. Snell, the landlord, recalled seeing a peddler who had called to drink at the Rainbow about a month before. This peddler had said that he carried a tinderbox about with him to light his pipe. Here, surely, was a clue to be followed. As can happen when memory is joined with new information, Mr. Snell began to remember a clear impression made on him by the peddler's look and speech. He had a "look with his eye" that fell unpleasantly on Mr. Snell. To be sure, he didn't say anything particular—except about the tinderbox. But it isn't what a man says, it's the way he says it. Besides, he had a foreign look about him that showed little honesty.

Some disappointment was felt after Silas Marner was questioned by the Squire and the rector. Silas had no other recollection of the peddler other than that he had called at his door, but had not entered his house. He turned away after Silas said that he wanted nothing. This had been Silas's testimony, though he clutched at the idea of the peddler being the robber. It gave him a definite image of the whereabouts of his gold. He could see it now in the peddler's box.

It was observed in the village, however, that any-

___

2. **rector** religious person in charge of a church parish

body but a "blind creature" like Marner would have seen the man prowling about. For how had he come to leave his tinderbox in the ditch close by, if he hadn't been lingering there? He had probably made his observations when he saw Marner at the door. Anybody might know by looking at him that the weaver was half crazy. It was a wonder the peddler hadn't murdered him.

Godfrey Cass entered the Rainbow during one of Mr. Snell's frequent descriptions of his testimony. Godfrey had treated it lightly, stating that he himself had bought a penknife from the peddler. He thought him a merry grinning fellow. It was all nonsense, he said, about the man's evil looks.

This was spoken of in the village as the random talk of youth. It was to be hoped Mr. Godfrey would not go to Tarley and throw cold water on what Mr. Snell said there. It might prevent the justice from drawing up a warrant.[3] He was suspected of this when he was seen setting off on horseback in the direction of Tarley.

By this time, however, Godfrey's interest in the robbery had faded. He was becoming more worried about Dunstan and Wildfire. He was going, not to Tarley, but to Batherley, unable to wait any longer for word about them. On the way, Godfrey saw a horse and rider approaching him. When he got closer, he could see that the rider was Bryce. The man had a disagreeable expression on his face.

"Well, Mr. Godfrey, that's a lucky brother of yours, that Master Dunsey, isn't he?"

"What do you mean?" said Godfrey hastily.

"Why, hasn't he been home yet?" Bryce said.

---

3. **warrant**   a paper that gives the authority to arrest someone

"Home? No. What has happened? What has he done with my horse?"

"Ah, I thought it was yours, though he pretended you had parted with it to him."

"Has he thrown him down and broken his knees?" Godfrey said.

"Worse than that," Bryce said. "You see, I'd made a bargain with him to buy the horse for 120. And what does he do but go flying at a hedge atop of a bank with a ditch before it. The horse had been dead a pretty good while when he was found. So, he hasn't been home since, has he?"

"Home? No," said Godfrey. "And he'd better keep away. Confound me for a fool! I might have known this would be the end of it."

"After I'd bargained for the horse, it did come into my head that he might be riding and selling the horse without your knowledge. For I didn't believe it was his own. I knew Master Dunsey was up to his tricks sometimes. But where can he be gone? He's not been to Batherley. He couldn't have been hurt, for he must have walked off."

"Hurt," said Godfrey bitterly. "He'll never be hurt. He's made to hurt other people."

"And so you did give him leave to sell the horse, eh?" Bryce said.

"Yes, I wanted to part with the horse. He was always a little too hard in the mouth for me," Godfrey said. "I was going to see after him. I thought some mischief had happened. I'll go back now," he added, turning the horse's head. He wished he could get rid of Bryce, for he feared that the long-dreaded crisis in his life was close upon him. "You're coming on to Raveloe, aren't you?"

"Well, no, not now," Bryce said. "I was coming round

there for I thought I might as well let you know all I knew about the horse. I suppose Master Dunsey didn't like to show himself until the news had blown over a bit."

Godfrey made an effort at carelessness. "We shall hear of him soon enough, I suppose," he said.

"Well, I'll bid you good day," Bryce said. "And wish I may bring you better news another time."

Godfrey rode along slowly. He imagined the scene of confession to his father, from which he felt there was no longer any escape. The truth about the money must be told the very next morning. If not, Dunstan would be sure to come back shortly and tell the whole story out of spite. There was one step, perhaps, by which he might still win Dunstan's silence. He might tell his father that he himself had spent the money Fowler paid him. As he had never done such a thing before, the affair would soon blow over. But Godfrey could not bend himself to this.

"I don't pretend to be a good fellow," he said to himself. "But I'm not a scoundrel. I will not make believe I have done what I never would have done. I'd never have spent the money for my own pleasure."

Through the rest of the day, Godfrey kept his will bent in the direction of telling his father the complete truth. If he let slip this one opportunity, he might never have another. The whole truth might be told in an even more horrible way than by Dunstan. Molly might come, as she had threatened to do. Still, there was just the chance, Godfrey thought, that his father's pride might see this marriage in a light that would cause him to hush it up. He might do that rather than turn his son out and make the family the talk of the country for 10 miles around.

This was the view that Godfrey managed to keep

before him almost till midnight. He went to sleep thinking he was done with inward debating. But when he awoke in the morning darkness, the old fear of disgrace came back. What would really be wisest for him to do was to try and soften his father's anger against Dunsey. He should try to keep things as nearly possible in their old condition. If Dunsey did not come back for a few days, everything might blow over.

Godfrey rose and took his own breakfast earlier than usual. Then he stayed in the parlor until his younger brothers had finished their meal and gone out. He was waiting for his father, who always went out and had a walk with his managing man before breakfast. Everyone had breakfast at a different hour in the Red House, and the Squire was always the latest.

The table had been set for two hours before he came for breakfast. The squire was a tall, stout man of 60, with a rather hard glance that was offset by his feeble mouth. He was untidy, and yet there was something about the Squire that distinguished him from the other farmers in the area. The Squire was used to the idea that everything that was his, from his family to his dishes, was the oldest and the best. Since he never saw anybody higher than himself, his opinion was not disturbed by comparison.

He glanced at his son as he entered the room. "What, sir! Haven't you had your breakfast yet?"

"Yes, sir," Godfrey said. "I've had my breakfast. But I was waiting to speak to you."

"Ah, well," said the Squire, throwing himself into his chair.

"There's been a cursed piece of ill luck with Wildfire," Godfrey began. "It happened the day before yesterday."

"What! Broke his knees?" said the Squire. "I thought you knew how to ride better than that. I never threw a horse down in my life. If I had, I might have whistled in vain for another. For my father wasn't quite so ready to buy a new one as some other fathers I know of. And what with mortgages and back rent due, I'm as short of cash as a roadside pauper. There's that damned Fowler, too. I won't put up with him any longer. The lying scoundrel told me he'd be sure to pay me 100 pounds last month. He takes advantage because he's on that outlying farm and thinks I shall forget him."

"It's worse than breaking the horse's knees," Godfrey went on. "He's been killed. But I wasn't asking you to buy me another horse. I was only thinking that I'd lost the means of paying you with the price of Wildfire, as I'd meant to do. Dunsey took him to the hunt to sell him for me the other day. After he'd made a bargain with Bryce, he took some fool's leap and killed the horse. If it hadn't been for that, I should have paid you 100 pounds."

The Squire stared at his son in amazement. He had no idea why Godfrey should owe him 100 pounds.

"The truth is, sir—I'm very sorry—I was quite to blame," Godfrey said. "Fowler did pay that 100 pounds. He paid it to me, when I was over there one day last month. Dunsey bothered me for the money, and I let him have it. I hoped I should be able to pay you back before this."

The Squire was purple with anger before his son had done speaking. "Let Dunsey have the money! Why should you let Dunsey have the money? There's some lie at the bottom of it."

"There's no lie, sir," Godfrey said. "I wouldn't have

spent the money myself, but Dunsey bothered me. And I was a fool and let him have it. But I meant to pay it, whether he did or not."

"Where's Dunsey, then? What do you stand there talking for? Go and fetch Dunsey."

"Dunsey hasn't come back, sir. I don't know where he is."

"And what must you be letting him have my money for? Answer me that," said the Squire.

"Well, sir, I don't know," Godfrey said.

"You don't know? I'll tell you what it is, sir. You've been up to some trick. And you've been bribing him not to tell." Godfrey felt his heart beat violently at the nearness of his father's guess.

"Why, sir, it was a little affair between me and Dunsey," he said, trying to speak with careless ease. "It's hardly worth while to pry into young men's fooleries. If I'd not had the bad luck to lose Wildfire, I should have paid you the money."

"Fooleries! It's time you were done with fooleries. And I'd have you know, sir, you must be done with them."

The Squire ate his bread and took a drink and began to speak again. "It will be all the worse for you, you know. You need to try and help me keep things together."

"Well, sir, I've often offered to take the management of things. But you seemed to think I wanted to push you out of your place."

"I know nothing of your offering," said the Squire. "But I know you seemed to be thinking of marrying. I didn't put any obstacles in your way, as some fathers would. I'd just as soon you marry Lammeter's daughter as anybody. I suppose if I had said no, you would have kept on with it. But since I didn't, you've changed your mind. You're a silly, shallow fellow. You take after your poor mother. She never had a will of her own. The lass hasn't said she wouldn't have you, has she?"

"No," said Godfrey. "But I don't think she will."

"Think! Why haven't you had the courage to ask her? Do you stick to it, do you want to have her? That's the thing."

"There's no other woman I want to marry," Godfrey said.

"Well, then, let me make the offer for you, if you haven't the pluck to do it yourself. Lammeter isn't likely to be against his daughter marrying into my family, I should think. As for the pretty lass, there's nobody else, as I see, to stand in your way."

"I'd rather let it be at present, sir," Godfrey said in alarm. "I think she's a little offended with me just now. And I should like to speak for myself. A man must manage these things for himself."

"Well, speak then and manage it. And see if you can't turn over a new leaf. That's what a man must do when he thinks of marrying."

"I don't see how I can think of it at present, sir. You wouldn't like to settle me on one of the farms, I suppose. And I don't think she'd come to live in this house with all my brothers."

"Not come to live in this house? You ask her, that's all," said the Squire with a short laugh.

"I'd rather let the thing be, at present, sir," Godfrey said. "I hope you won't try to hurry it on by saying anything."

"I shall do what I choose," said the Squire. "I shall let you know I'm master. Or else you may leave and find an estate to drop into somewhere else. Get that horse of Dunsey's sold and hand me the money, will you? He'll keep no more horses at my expense. And if you know where he's sneaking, you may tell him to spare himself the journey of coming back home. He shall not hang on me anymore."

"I don't know where he is, sir. And if I did, it isn't my place to tell him to keep away," Godfrey said, moving toward the door.

"Confound it, sir, don't stay arguing. Do what I say."

Godfrey left the room. He was relieved that the discussion was ended without his position being changed. At the same time, he was uneasy because he had entangled himself in still more lies and deceit.

Chapter 5

Justice Malam was thought in Tarley and Raveloe to be a man with a wide-open mind. Such a man was not likely to neglect the clue of the tinderbox. An inquiry[1] was set concerning a peddler, name unknown, with curly black hair and a foreign complexion. But perhaps the inquiry was too slow-footed to find him. The description may have applied to so many peddlers that it was difficult to choose among them. Weeks passed away. There was no other result concerning the robbery other than the gradual ending of the excitement it had caused in Raveloe.

Dunstan Cass's absence was hardly a subject of remark. He had once before had a quarrel with his father and had gone off, nobody knew where, and then returned at the end of six weeks and taken up his old life. This time, the Squire determined to ban him. To connect the fact that Dunstan disappeared on the same day of the robbery was far from the track of everyone's thought. Godfrey had better reason than anyone to know what his brother could do. Yet, his mind saw Dunstan off in some place living off the people he might come across. He felt Dunstan would return home sooner or later to the old amusement of tormenting his elder brother.

Silas was feeling the awful loneliness of mourning for his gold. The loom was still there, and the weaving and the growing pattern in the cloth. But the bright treasure in the hole under his feet was gone. The prospect of handling and counting it was gone. The

---

1. **inquiry** investigation

evening had no fantasy of delight to still the poor soul's craving. The thought of the money he would get by his actual work could bring no joy. Its small image was only a fresh reminder of his loss. Hope was too heavily crushed for his imagination to count on the growth of a new pile from that small beginning.

Yet, he was not utterly forgotten in his trouble. The disgust Marner had always created in his neighbors was partly swept away by the new light in which this misfortune had shown him. Before, Marner was thought to have more cunning than honest folks could come by. Worse, he never thought to use that cunning in a neighborly way. Now, it was clear that Silas had not enough cunning to keep his own. He was generally spoken of as a "poor mushed creature." Before, his avoiding his neighbors had been thought a result of his ill will. Now, it was considered mere craziness.

This change to a kinder feeling was shown in various ways. The smell of Christmas cooking was in the wind. One Sunday, Mrs. Winthrop, the wheelwright's[2] wife, took her little boy Aaron with her, and went to call on Silas. Mrs. Winthrop was a very mild, patient woman. She was the person always first thought of in Raveloe when there was an illness or death in a family.

When she and Aaron went to call on Silas, she carried in her hand some small lard cakes. They were flat, pastelike articles, much valued in Raveloe. When mother and son arrived at the Stone Pits, they heard the mysterious sound of the loom.

"Ah, it is as I thought," Mrs. Winthrop said, sadly.

They had to knock loudly before Silas heard them. When he came to the door he showed no impatience, as he would once have done at an unasked-for visit.

---

2. **wheelwright** maker and repairer of vehicles with wheels

Before, his heart had been locked, with its treasure inside. Now, it was empty, and the lock broken. He opened the door wide to admit Dolly. He did not return her greeting. But he moved an armchair a few inches as a sign that she was to sit down in it. As soon as she was seated, Dolly removed the white cloth that covered her lard cakes.

"I was baking yesterday, Master Marner, and the lard cakes turned out better than usual. I ask you to accept some. I don't eat such things myself. A bit of bread is what I like from one end of the year to the other. But men's stomachs are made different."

Dolly sighed gently as she held out the cakes to Silas. He looked very closely at them, without thinking. He was used to looking closely at everything he took into his hand.

"Thank you, thank you kindly," he said. He laid down the cakes and seated himself, again without thinking.

Dolly looked at Silas with pity as she went on. "But you didn't hear the church bells this morning, Master Marner? I doubt you didn't know it was Sunday. Living so alone here, you lose your count. And then, when your loom makes a noise, you can't hear the bells."

"Yes, I did. I heard them," Silas said. But Sunday bells were a mere accident of the day, not part of its sacredness. There had been no bells in Lantern Yard.

"Dear heart!" Dolly said. "But what a pity it is you should work on a Sunday and not clean yourself. But now, upon Christmas day, if you was to go to church and see the holly, you'd be a deal the better."

"Nay, nay," he said. "I know nothing of church. I've never been to church."

"No!" said Dolly, in a low tone of wonderment. "Could it have been they had no church where you were born?"

"Oh, yes," said Silas. "There were many churches. It was a big town. But I knew nothing of them. I went to chapel."

Dolly was very puzzled at this new world. But she was afraid to ask anything further, for fear that chapel meant some place of wickedness. After a little thought, she spoke again.

"Well, Master Marner, it's never too late to turn over a new leaf. And if you've never been to church, there's no telling the good it will do you."

Silas remained silent. He wasn't about to agree that he should go to church.

"We must be going home now," Dolly said, after a while. "And so I wish you good-bye, Master Marner. And if you ever feel bad in your inside, and you can't fend for yourself, I'll come and clean up for you, and get you a bit of food. But I beg of you to leave off weaving on a Sunday. It's bad for soul and body. And the money that comes in that way will be a bad bed to lie down on at the last, if it doesn't fly away. And you'll excuse me for being that free with you, Master Marner. I wish you well, I do. Make your bow, Aaron."

And so, despite the honest persuasions of a neighbor like Dolly Winthrop, Silas spent his Christmas day in loneliness. He ate his meal in sadness of heart. Nobody in this world but he knew he was the same Silas Marner who had once loved his fellow man with tender love. He was the same Silas Marner who had once trusted in an unseen goodness. Even to himself, that past had become dim.

In Raveloe village, however, the bells rang merrily. The church was fuller than all through the rest of the year. At Squire Cass's party that day, nobody mentioned Dunstan. Nobody was sorry for his absence or feared it would be too long. But the party on

Christmas day was strictly a family party. It was not the brilliant celebration of the season at the Red House.

It was the great dance on New Year's Eve that was the glory of Squire Cass. This was the occasion when all the society of Raveloe and Tarley came together for a feast.

Godfrey Cass was looking forward to this New Year's Eve with a foolish longing. It made him half deaf to his constant companion, Anxiety.

"Dunsey will be coming home soon. There will be a great blowup. And how will you bribe him to silence?" said Anxiety.

"Oh, he won't come home before New Year's Eve, perhaps," Godfrey said. "And I shall sit by Nancy then and dance with her. I will get a kind look from her in spite of herself."

"But money is wanted in another quarter," said Anxiety in a louder voice. "And how will you get it without selling your mother's diamond pin? And if you don't get it...?"

"Well, but something may happen to make things easier. At any rate, there's one pleasure for me close at hand. Nancy is coming."

"Yes, and suppose your father should bring matters to a pass. Then you must decline marrying her and give your reasons."

"Hold your tongue, and don't worry me. I can see Nancy's eyes, just as they will look at me. I feel her hand in mine already."

But Anxiety went on, though in noisy Christmas company. It refused to be utterly silenced, even by much drinking.

Chapter 6

Some women, I admit, would not appear at an advantage seated on a pillion[1] and dressed in a drab cloak and drab bonnet. It was a great triumph to Miss Nancy Lammeter's beauty that she looked so bewitching in that costume. She was seated on the pillion behind her father and held one arm around him. She looked down. Below, the snow-covered puddles sent up splashes of mud under the horse's foot. As they arrived at the door of the Red House, she saw Mr. Godfrey Cass. He came forward, ready to lift her from the pillion.

Nancy wished her sister Priscilla had come up at the same time. Then she would have arranged that Mr. Godfrey should have lifted off Priscilla first. In the meantime, she would have persuaded her father to go round to the horse block instead of at the doorsteps.

It was very painful for Nancy to see Mr. Godfrey Cass. She had made it quite clear that she was determined not to marry him, however much he might wish it. Still, he continued to pay her marked attention. Why didn't he always show the same attentions, if he meant them sincerely? Instead, he acted strange. Sometimes he behaved as if he didn't want to speak to her. He took no notice of her for weeks and weeks. And then, all of a sudden, he was wooing her again.

It was quite plain that he had no real love for her. Or else he would not let people say what they did about him. Did he suppose that Miss Nancy Lammeter was to be won by any man, squire or no squire, who

---

1. pillion pad or cushion placed behind a horse saddle

had led a bad life? That was not what she was used to in her own father. He was the best man in the country.

All these thoughts ran through Nancy's mind at her first sight of Mr. Godfrey Cass. Happily, the Squire came out, too. He gave a loud greeting to her father. Under the cover of this noise, she was able to hide her confusion as Godfrey lifted her from the pillion. And then there was a good reason to go inside, as snow was beginning to fall. As she entered the house, Mrs. Kimble came forward to meet her in the hall. Mrs. Kimble was the Squire's sister as well as the doctor's wife. On these great occasions, she did the honors at the Red House.

As soon as Nancy made her greeting, an elderly woman came forward. "Niece, I hope I see you well in health," she said to Nancy. Nancy kissed her aunt's cheek. "Quite well, I thank you, Aunt. And I hope I see you the same."

These questions and answers were continued until several things were learned. The Lammeters were as well as usual, and the Osgoods likewise. The niece Priscilla must certainly arrive shortly.

In a little while, sister Priscilla entered. After the first questions and greetings, she turned to Nancy. She looked her over from head to foot.

"What do you think of these gowns, Aunt Osgood?" Priscilla said, while Nancy helped her dress.

"Very handsome indeed, niece," said Mrs. Osgood.

"I'm obliged to have the same as Nancy, you know. I'm five years older and it makes me look yellow. But she never will have anything without me having one just like it. She wants us to look like sisters. But folks will think it's my weakness that makes me think that I shall look pretty in what she looks pretty in. For I am ugly, there's no denying that."

Nancy felt an inward flutter that no inner stern-
ness could prevent when she saw Mr. Godfrey Cass
coming toward her. He came to lead her to a seat
between himself and Mr. Crackenthorp. It did matter
to Nancy that the love she had given up was the most
important young man in the region. It deepened her
resolve that the most dazzling rank would not cause
her to marry a man of uncertain character. Nancy was
capable of keeping her word to herself under very trying conditions. Nothing but a blush betrayed the
thoughts she felt.

"Ha, Miss Nancy," Mr. Crackenthorp said, smiling
pleasantly at her. "When anybody says this has been a
severe winter, I shall tell them I saw the roses bloom-
ing on New Year's Eve. Eh, Godfrey, what do you say?"

Godfrey made no reply and avoided looking at
Nancy. But the Squire was rather impatient at
Godfrey's silence. He felt it was his duty to be jovial.
He wished to make up for his son's silence by speaking
for him.

"Ay, ay, us old fellows may wish ourselves young
tonight," he began. "It's true most things have gone
backward in the last 30 years. The country's going
down since the old king fell ill. But when I look at Miss
Nancy here, I begin to think the lasses keep up their
quality."

"Miss Nancy's wonderful like her mother was, isn't
she, Kimble," said the stout lady of that name. She
looked around for her husband.

Doctor Kimble had been roaming around the room
speaking with many of his female patients. Now he
skipped to Nancy's side. "Miss Nancy, you won't forget
your promise? You're to save a dance for me."

"Come, come, Kimble, don't you be too forward,"
said the Squire. "Give the young ones fair play. My son

Godfrey will be wanting to have a round with you if you run off with Miss Nancy. He's asked her for the first dance, I'm sure. Eh, sir! What do you say?" he continued, looking at Godfrey. "Haven't you asked Miss Nancy to open the dance with you?"

Godfrey was very uncomfortable, but he saw no course open but to turn and say something to Nancy.

"No, I've not asked her yet. But I hope she'll consent, if somebody else hasn't asked before me."

"No, I've not engaged myself," said Nancy quietly. (If Mr. Godfrey found any hopes in her agreeing to dance with him, he was mistaken. But there was no need for her to be rude.)

"Then I hope you have no objections to dancing with me," Godfrey said.

"No, no objections," said Nancy, coldly.

"Ah, well, you're a lucky fellow, Godfrey," said Doctor Kimble. "But you're my godson, so I won't stand in your way."

Squire Cass called for the fiddler to come in. Solomon Macey, an old man with white hair, walked in, fiddling as he walked. He bowed to the Squire and the rector.

"I hope I see your honor and your reverence well," Solomon said. "I wish you a happy New Year."

As Solomon spoke the last words, he bowed in all directions. Then, he began to play a tune.

"Ay, ay, Solomon, we know what that means," said the Squire, rising. "It's time to begin the dance, eh? Lead the way, then, and we'll all follow you."

Solomon marched forward at the head of the crowd into the White Parlor. Solomon's brother, the tailor Mr. Macey, and a few other villagers were allowed to watch on these great occasions. They were seated on benches placed near the door. The crowd was pleased and satisfied when the couples formed for the dance. The Squire led off with Mrs. Crackenthorp, and they joined hands with the rector and Mrs. Osgood.

"The Squire is pretty spry, considering his weight," Mr. Macey said to Ben Winthrop.

"Talk of nimbleness, look at Mrs. Osgood," said Ben. "It's as if she had little wheels on her feet. She doesn't look a day older than last year."

"Hey, by jingo, there's the young Squire, leading off now, with Miss Nancy for partners!" Ben went on. "There's a lass for you! There's nobody would think a lass could be so pretty. I shouldn't wonder if she's Madam Cass someday, after all. They make a fine match. You can find nothing against Master Godfrey's shape, Macey. I'll bet a penny."

"Huh!" said Mr. Macey. "He hasn't come into his right color yet. And I'm sure he's got a soft place in his head. Or else why would he let himself be turned around the finger of that rubbish Dunsey, who nobody has seen of late? Once he was always after Miss Nancy. And then it was all off again. That wasn't my way."

"Well, perhaps Miss Nancy hung off, and your lass didn't," Ben said.

"I should say she didn't," Mr. Macey replied.

"Well, I think Miss Nancy's coming round again," Ben said. "Master Godfrey doesn't look so downhearted tonight. And I see he's taking her away to sit down. That looks like sweethearting, that does."

The reason Godfrey and Nancy had left the dance was not so tender as Ben imagined. The bottom of Nancy's dress had become caught under the stamp of the Squire's foot. This caused certain stitches at the waist to come apart. Nancy had said to Godfrey with a deep blush that she must go and sit down until Priscilla could come to her. The sisters had already exchanged a short whisper.

Only a reason this urgent could have caused Nancy to give Godfrey this opportunity of sitting apart with her. As for Godfrey, he was feeling very happy under the charm of the long country dance with Nancy. He became bold on the strength of her confusion and led her, without being asked, into the small parlor where the card tables were set.

"Oh, no, thank you," said Nancy coldly, when she saw where he was going. "Not in there. I'll wait here until Priscilla's ready to come to me. I'm sorry to bring you out of that dance and make myself troublesome."

"Why, you'll be more comfortable here by yourself," Godfrey said. He spoke as if what she did was of no matter to him. "I'll leave you until your sister comes."

That was just what Nancy wanted. Then why was she a little hurt that Mr. Godfrey should suggest it? They entered, and she seated herself.

"Thank you, sir," she said. "I won't give you any more trouble. I'm sorry you had such an unlucky partner."

"That's very ill-natured of you, to be sorry you've danced with me," Godfrey said.

"Oh, no, sir. I don't mean to say what's ill-natured at all," Nancy said. "When gentlemen have so many pleasures, one dance can matter very little."

"You know that isn't true. You know one dance with you matters more to me than all the other pleasures in the world."

It had been a long while since Godfrey had said anything so direct as that. Nancy was startled. But she sat perfectly still. And she threw a little more decision into her voice.

"No, indeed, Mr. Godfrey, that's not known to me," Nancy said. "And I have very good reasons for thinking different. But if it's true, I don't wish to hear it."

"Would you never forgive me, then, Nancy?" Godfrey said. "Would you never think the present made up for the past? Not if I turned into a good fellow and gave up everything you didn't like?"

Godfrey was aware that this sudden opportunity to speak to Nancy alone had caused his feelings for her to get the better of his tongue. Nancy felt very stirred up by what Godfrey's words suggested, but this feeling called up all her powers of self-command.

"I should be glad to see a good change in anybody, Mr. Godfrey," she answered. "But it would be better if no change was needed."

"You're very hardhearted, Nancy," Godfrey said. "You might encourage me to be a better fellow. I'm very miserable, and you've no feeling."

"I think those that have the least feeling are those that act wrong to begin with," Nancy said. She sent out a slight flash of anger in spite of herself. Godfrey was delighted with that little flash. He would have liked to go on and make her quarrel with him. Nancy was so quiet and firm that it frustrated him.

Priscilla then entered, bustling forward. "Dear heart alive, child, let us look at this gown," she cried. And this cut off Godfrey's hopes for a quarrel.

"I suppose I must go now," he said to Priscilla.

"It's no matter to me whether you go or stay," said Priscilla.

"Do you want me to go?" Godfrey said, looking at Nancy.

"As you like," Nancy said, trying to recover all her former coldness.

"Then I'd like to stay," Godfrey said. He was determined to get as much of this joy as he could tonight and think nothing of tomorrow.

Chapter 7

While Godfrey Cass was enjoying the sweet presence of Nancy, Godfrey's wife, Molly, was walking with slow, uncertain steps through the snow-covered Raveloe lanes. She was carrying her child in her arms.

This journey on New Year's Eve was a planned act of vengeance. Molly had kept it in her heart ever since Godfrey had told her he would sooner die than acknowledge her as his wife. There would be a great party at the Red House on New Year's Eve, she knew. Her husband would be smiling and smiled upon. And he would be hiding her existence in the darkest corner of his heart.

She would ruin his pleasure, however. She would go in her dirty rags, with her faded face, once as handsome as the best. She would go with her little child that had its father's hair and eyes. And then she'd reveal herself to the Squire as his eldest son's wife.

Molly knew that the cause of her dirty rags was not her husband's neglect. The cause was the demon Opium.[1] She was a slave to it, body and soul, except in a mother's tenderness that refused to give him her hungry child. She knew this well. Yet, she felt bitterness towards Godfrey. *He* was well off. And if she had her rights, she would be well off, too.

She had set out at an early hour. But she had believed that if she waited under a warm shed, the snow would stop. She had waited longer than she knew. It was seven o'clock, and by this time she was not very far from Raveloe. But she was not familiar

---

1. **Opium** addictive drug made from poppies

enough with the lanes to know how near she was to her journey's end.

She needed comfort, and she knew only one comforter—the familiar demon in her pocket. She drew out the liquid and raised it to her lips. A moment later, she had flung the empty bottle away. Then she walked on again, always more and more sleepily. She clutched closer and closer the sleeping child to her chest.

Slowly, the demon was working his will. Cold and weariness were his helpers. Soon she felt nothing but a strong longing to lie down and sleep. She sank down against a straggling bush, an easy pillow enough. The bed of snow, too, was soft. She did not feel that the bed was cold. She did not know if the child would wake and cry for her. Her arms had not yet relaxed their mother's clutch. The little one slept on as gently as if it had been rocked in a cradle.

Complete sleep came at last. The fingers lost their tension, the arms unbent. Then the little head fell away from the chest. The blue eyes opened wide on the cold starlight. There was a cry of "Mammy" and an effort to keep the pillow of arm and chest. But mammy's ear was deaf, and the pillow seemed to be slipping away backward.

The child rolled downward on its mother's knees, all wet with snow. Suddenly, its eyes were caught by a bright glancing light on the white ground. In an instant, the child had slipped on all fours and held out one little hand to catch the gleam. But the gleam would not be caught in that way. Now, the head was held up to see where the gleam came from.

It came from a very bright place. And the little one, rising on its legs, toddled through the snow. The old grimy shawl in which it was wrapped trailed behind it. It toddled on to the open door of Silas Marner's cottage. It went right up to the warm hearth, where there was a bright fire of logs and sticks. The fire had thoroughly warmed the old sack[2] spread out on the bricks to dry.

The little one was used to being left to itself for long hours without notice from its mother. It squatted down on the sack and spread its tiny hands toward the blaze. It was perfectly content, gurgling to the cheerful fire.

Where was Silas Marner when this strange visitor had come to his hearth? He was in the cottage, but he did not see the child. Since he had lost his money, he had begun the habit of opening his door and looking out from time to time. It was as if he thought that his money might be somehow coming back to him. It was chiefly at night, when he was not at his loom, that he fell into this act. It can only be understood by those who have undergone a bewildering separation from a much-loved object.

This morning he had been told by some of his neighbors that it was New Year's Eve. They said he must sit up and hear the old year rung out and the new rung in. That was good luck, and it might bring his money back. This was only a friendly Raveloe way of jesting with the half-crazy miser. But it had perhaps helped to throw Silas into an unusually excited state.

Since twilight, he had opened his door again and again. Each time he shut it immediately at seeing everything covered by the falling snow. The last time he opened it, the snow had stopped. He stood and listened and gazed for a long while. There was really something on the road coming toward him then. But he caught no sight of it.

---

2. **sack** loose-fitting coat

He went in again and put his right hand on the door latch to close it. But he did not close it. Instead, he went into one of his trances. He stood with sightless eyes, holding open his door, powerless to resist either the good or evil that might enter there.

When Marner's senses returned, he continued what he had been doing before his trance. He closed the door. He turned toward the hearth where the two logs had fallen apart. He seated himself on his fireside chair and stooped to push his logs together. Then, to his blurred vision, it seemed as if there were gold on the floor in front of the hearth. Gold! His own gold brought back to him as mysteriously as it had been taken away!

He felt his heart begin to beat violently. For a few moments he was unable to stretch out his hand and grasp the restored treasure. He leaned forward at last and stretched forth his hand. But instead of the hard coin, his fingers felt soft, warm curls. In utter amazement, Silas bent forward to examine it. It was a sleeping child—a round, fair thing, with soft yellow rings all over its head. Could this be his little sister come back to him in a dream? Could it be the little sister whom he had carried about in his arms for a year before she died when he was a small boy?

That was the first thought that darted across Silas's blank mind. Was it a dream? He rose to his feet again. He pushed his logs together, threw on some dried leaves and sticks, and raised a flame. But the flame did not make the vision disappear.

How and when had the child come in without his knowledge? He had never been beyond the door. There was a vision of his old home and the streets leading to Lantern Yard. He had a dreamy feeling that the child was a message from that far-off life.

A moment later, there was a cry on the hearth. The child had awakened. Marner stooped to lift it on his knee. It clung round his neck and burst louder and louder into cries of "Mammy." Silas pressed it to him, and uttered sounds of hushing tenderness.

He had plenty to do through the next hour. He got some porridge and sweetened it with some dry brown sugar. It stopped the cries of the little one. And it made her lift her blue eyes with a wide quiet gaze at Silas as he fed her. Soon she slipped from his knee and began to toddle about. She fell in a sitting position on the ground, and began to pull at her boots. She looked up at him with a crying face as if the boots hurt her. It occurred to Silas that the wet boots were the problem, pressing on her warm ankles. He got them off with difficulty, and baby was at once happy.

The wet boots had at last suggested to Silas that the child had been walking on the snow. He raised the child in his arms, and went to the door. As soon as he had opened it, there was the cry of "Mammy" again. Bending forward, he could just make out the marks made by the little feet on the snow. He followed their tracks to the bushes. "Mammy!" the little one cried again and again. Silas then became aware that there was something more than the bush before him. There was a human body, with the head sunk low in the bush and half-covered with the shaken snow.

Early suppertime at the Red House had ended. The entertainment was in that stage when bashfulness had passed into easy laughter. At this point of the evening, the heavy duties of supper were well over. It was usual for the servants to get their share of amusement by coming to look on at the dancing. The back regions of the house were left empty.

Godfrey's brother Bob Cass was dancing a horn-pipe.³ Godfrey was standing a little way off, but not to admire his brother's dancing. He was keeping sight of Nancy, who was seated in the group near her father. Godfrey lifted his eyes from one of those long glances at Nancy. And his eyes met an object as startling to him as if it had been a ghost. It was his own child, carried in Silas Marner's arms. That was his first sure impression, though he had not seen the child for months.

He briefly held a rising hope that he might be mistaken. But Mr. Crackenthorp and Mr. Lammeter had already advanced to Silas, astonished at this strange event. Godfrey joined them right away, unable to resist hearing every word. He tried to control himself. But he was aware that he was white-lipped and trembling.

Now all eyes were bent on Silas Marner. The Squire himself had risen and asked angrily, "How's this? What's this? What do you do coming in here this way?"

"I've come for the doctor. I want the doctor." Silas had said in the first moment to Mr. Crackenthorp.

"Why, what's the matter, Marner?" said the rector. "The doctor's here. But say quietly why you want him."

"It's a woman," Silas speaking low, just as Godfrey came up. "She's dead, I think. Dead in the snow at the Stone Pits not far from my door."

Godfrey felt a great throb. There was one terror in his mind at that moment: it was that the woman might not be dead.

"Hush, hush!" said Mr. Crackenthorp. "Go out into the hall there. I'll fetch the doctor to you. Found a woman in the snow. And thinks she's dead," he added, speaking low to the Squire. "Say as little about it as

3. **hornpipe** a lively British folk dance

possible. It will shock the ladies. Just tell them a poor woman is ill from cold and hunger. I'll go and fetch Kimble."

By this time, however, the ladies had pressed forward. They were curious to know what could have brought the weaver there. And they were interested in the pretty child.

"What child is it?" said several ladies at once. And among the rest, Nancy Lammeter addressed Godfrey.

"I don't know. Some poor woman who's been found in the snow, I believe," Godfrey said. He had wrung the answer from himself with a terrible effort.

"Well, you'd better leave the child here, Master Marner," said the good-natured Mrs. Kimble. "I'll tell one of the girls to fetch it."

"No, no. I can't part with it. I can't let it go," Silas said abruptly. "It's come to me. I've got a right to keep it."

Silas surprised himself with his speech. A minute before he had no clear intention about the child.

"Did you ever hear the like?" said Mrs. Kimble, in mild surprise, to her neighbor.

"Now, ladies, I must trouble you to stand aside," said Doctor Kimble, coming from the card room.

He quickly left with Marner and was followed by Mr. Crackenthorp and Godfrey. "Get me a pair of thick boots, Godfrey, will you?" Kimble said. "And let someone run to Winthrop's and fetch Dolly. She's the best woman to get. Ben was here himself before supper. Is he gone?"

"Yes, sir, I met him," said Marner. "I couldn't stop to tell him anything. I only said I was going for the doctor. He said the doctor was at the Squire's. I made haste."

Godfrey had come back with the boots. "I'll go and

fetch the woman, Mrs. Winthrop," he said.

"Oh, send somebody else," said Uncle Kimble, hurrying away with Marner.

"You let me know if I can be of any use, Kimble," Mr. Crackenthorp said. But the doctor was out of hearing.

In a few minutes Godfrey was on his rapid way to the Stone Pits by the side of Dolly. "You better go back, sir," Dolly said. "You've no call to catch cold."

"No, I'll stay now, once I'm out. I'll stay outside here," Godfrey said, when they came opposite Marner's cottage. "You can tell me if I can do anything."

"Well, sir, you're very good. You've got a tender heart," said Dolly, going to the door.

Godfrey walked up and down, not aware that he was plunging ankle deep in snow. "Is she dead?" said the voice within him. "If she is, I may marry Nancy. And then I shall be a good fellow in the future and have no secrets. And the child shall be taken care of somehow." But across that vision came the other possibility. "She may live. And then it's all over with me."

Godfrey never knew how long it was before the cottage door opened and Doctor Kimble came out. He went forward to meet his uncle. "I waited for you, as I'd come so far," Godfrey said.

"It was nonsense for you to come out," Kimble said. "There's nothing to be done. She's dead—has been dead for hours, I should say."

"What sort of woman is she?" Godfrey said, feeling the blood rush to his face.

"A young woman, very thin, with long black hair. Some vagrant⁴ dressed in rags. She's got a wedding ring on, however. Come, come along."

"I want to look at her," Godfrey said. "I think I saw

---

4. vagrant homeless wanderer

such a woman yesterday. I'll overtake you in a minute or two."

Doctor Kimble went on. Godfrey went back to the cottage. He cast only one glance at the dead face on the pillow. But he remembered that last look on his unhappy, hated wife well. Every line in the worn face was present to him 16 years later when he told the full story of the night.

He turned right away toward the hearth. Silas Marner sat there lulling the child. She was perfectly quiet.

"You'll take the child to the parish tomorrow?" Godfrey asked, as casually as he could.

"Who says so?" said Marner, sharply. "Will they make me take her?"

"Why, you wouldn't like to keep her, should you? An old bachelor like you?"

"Till anybody shows they have a right to take her away from me," Marner said. "The mother's dead. And I reckon it's got no father. It's a lone thing, and I'm a lone thing. My money's gone, I don't know where. And this has come from I don't know where. I'm partly amazed."

"Poor little thing," Godfrey said. "Let me give something toward finding it clothes."

He put his hand in his pocket and found half a guinea. He thrust it into Silas's hand. Then he hurried out of the cottage to overtake Doctor Kimble.

"Ah, I see it's not the same woman I saw," he said as he came up. "It's a pretty little child. The old fellow seems to want to keep it. That's strange for a miser like him. But I gave him a trifle to help him out. The parish isn't likely to quarrel with him to keep the child."

Godfrey reappeared in the White Parlor with a

sense of relief and gladness. There was no danger that his dead wife would be recognized. As for the record of their marriage, it was buried in unturned pages. Dunsey might betray him if he came back. But Dunsey might be won to silence.

Where would be the use of confessing his past to Nancy Lammeter? He would throw away his happiness and hers. For he felt some confidence that she loved him. As for the child, he would see that it was cared for. It might be just as happy in life without being owned by its father. Nobody could tell how things would turn out. And are there any other reasons wanted? Well then, the father would be much happier without owning the child.

Chapter 8

There was a pauper's burial that week in Raveloe, and in Batherley it was known that the dark-haired woman with the fair child who had been lodging there had gone away again. That was the only note taken that Molly had disappeared from the eyes of men. But that death, which seemed unimportant to most, was charged with changing certain lives we know of. It shaped their joys and sorrows to the end.

Silas's determination to keep the child was as much of a surprise and caused as much talk as the robbery of his money. Before, there had been a softening of feeling toward him which dated from his misfortune. Now, it came with a more active sympathy, especially among the women.

Among the mothers, Dolly Winthrop was the one whose suggestions were the most acceptable to Marner. Silas had shown her the half-guinea given to him by Godfrey. And he had asked her what he should do about getting some clothes for the child.

"Eh, Master Marner, there's no call to buy more than a pair of shoes," Dolly said. "I've got the little petticoats Aaron wore five years ago. It's bad spending money on them baby clothes. For the child will grow like grass in May—that it will."

The same day Dolly brought her bundle. She displayed to Marner the tiny garments. Most of them were patched and darned, but clean and neat.

"Anybody would think the angels in heaven couldn't be prettier," Dolly said, looking at the child. She rubbed the girl's golden curls and kissed them. "And to think of its being covered with them dirty rags," Dolly went on. "And the poor mother, froze to death. But there were those that took care of it, and brought it to your door, Master Marner. The door was open, and it walked in over the snow, like a starved robin. Didn't you say the door was open?"

"Yes," said Silas, thoughtfully. "Yes, the door was open. The money's gone, I don't know where. And this has come from I don't know where."

He had not mentioned to anyone that he was unaware of the child's entrance. He didn't want to answer questions that might lead to what he himself suspected—that he had been in one of his trances.

"I think you're right to keep the little one, Master Marner," Dolly said. "It's been sent to you. Though there are folks that think differently. You'll be a bit bothered with it while it's so little. But I'll come and see to the child for you. I've got bits of time to spare most days."

"Thank you...kindly," Silas said, hesitating a little. "I'll be glad if you tell me things. But I want to do things for it myself. Or else it may get fond of somebody else and not fond of me. I've been used to fending for myself in the house. I can learn, I can learn."

"To be sure," Dolly said gently.

Marner took the child on his lap. He was trembling with a mysterious emotion. Something unknown was dawning on his life. Thought and feeling were confused within him. If he had tried to state them, he could only have said that the child had come instead of the gold. The gold had turned into the child. He took the clothing from Dolly. And he put them on under her teaching.

"There, then! Why, you take to it quite easy, Master Marner," Dolly said. "But what shall you do when you're forced to sit at your loom?"

Silas thought for a little while. "I'll tie her to the leg of the loom," he said at last. "Tie her with a good long strip of something."

"Well, perhaps that will do," Dolly said. "A little girl will more easily sit in one place than will the lads. I know what the lads are. I've had four. I'll bring you my little chair and some bits of red rag for her to play with. And she'll sit and chatter to them as if they were alive. I should have been glad if one of my lads was a little girl. I could have taught her to clean and mend and knit and everything. But I can teach this little one, Master Marner, when she gets old enough."

"But she'll be *my* little one," Marner said rather hastily. "She'll be nobody else's."

"No, to be sure. You'll have a right to her if you're a father to her. But," Dolly added, "you must bring her up like christened folks' children. You must take her to church."

Marner's pale face flushed suddenly under a new worry. His mind was too busy trying to understand Dolly's words for him to think of answering her.

"And it's my belief, since the poor little creature has never been christened, that the parson should be spoken to. If you were willing, I'd talk to Mr. Macey about it this very day," Dolly went on.

Silas was puzzled and anxious. Dolly's word "christened" had no clear meaning to him. He had only heard of baptism. And he had only seen the baptism of grown-up men and women.

"What is it that you mean by 'christened?'" he said. "Won't folks be good to her without it?"

"Dear, dear, Master Marner," said Dolly gently. "Didn't you ever have a mother or father who taught you to say your prayers? And there's good words and good things to keep us from harm?"

"Yes," said Silas, in a low voice. "I know a good deal about them that used to. But your ways are different. My country was a good way off." He paused for a few moments. "But I want to do everything that can be done for the child. And whatever is right for it in this country, I'll do."

"Well, then, Master Marner, I'll ask Mr. Macey to speak to the parson about it. And you fix a name on it. Because it must have a name when it's christened."

"My mother's name was Hephzibah," Silas said. "And my little sister was named after her."

"That's a hard name," Dolly said. "I think it isn't a christened name."

"It's a Bible name," Silas said.

"Then I've no call to speak against it," Dolly answered. "But it was awkward calling your little sister by such a hard name, wasn't it?"

"We called her Eppie," Silas said.

"Well, it would be a deal handier. And so I'll go now, Master Marner. I'll speak about the christening before dark. And I wish you the best of luck. And it's my belief it will come to you if you do what's right by the orphan child."

The baby was christened. On this occasion Silas made himself clean and tidy and appeared for the first time within the church. He was quite unable, by any means, to identify the Raveloe religion with his old faith.

As the weeks grew to months, the child created fresh links between Silas's life and the lives of his neighbors. Unlike the gold that needed nothing, Eppie was a creature of endless claims and growing desires. The gold had kept Silas's thoughts in an ever-repeated circle, leading to nothing beyond itself. But Eppie was an object full of changes and hopes that forced Silas's thoughts onward. The gold had asked that Silas should sit weaving longer and longer. But Eppie called Silas away from his weaving. She made him think that all its pauses were a holiday. She warmed him into joy because *she* had joy. As the child's mind grew into knowledge, Silas's mind was growing into memory. As her life was unfolding, his soul was unfolding, too.

Silas took the child with him on most of his journeys to the farmhouses. Little curly-haired Eppie became an object of interest everywhere. Silas was met with open smiling faces and cheerful questioning. He was treated as a person whose satisfactions and difficulties could be understood. Everywhere, he was obliged to sit and talk about the child. And words of interest were always ready for him.

"Ah, Master Marner, you'll be lucky if she takes the measles soon and easy!" Or, "Why, there isn't many lone men would be willing to take up with a little one like that. But the weaving makes you handier than men who do outdoor work. You're almost as handy as a woman."

No child was afraid of approaching Silas when Eppie was near him. There was no disgust around him now, with young or old. The little child had come to link him once more with the whole world. There was love between him and the child that blended them into one.

By the time Eppie was three years old, she developed a fine capacity for mischief. This sorely puzzled poor Silas. Dolly Winthrop told him a good spanking now and then was good for Eppie. "To be sure, there's another thing you might do," added Dolly. "You might shut her in once in the coal-hole. That was what I did with Aaron. Master Marner, you must chose—either smacking or the coal-hole—else there will be no holding her."

Silas's force of mind failed him, though. It was painful for him to hurt Eppie. He trembled at the idea that she might love him the less for it.

He had chosen a broad strip of linen to fasten her to the loom when he was busy. One bright morning, Silas left his scissors on a ledge where Eppie's arm could reach. Like a mouse, she stole quietly from her corner, got the scissors, and toddled to the bed again. There, she cut the linen strip in two, and in moments had run out the open door, where the sunshine was inviting her.

It was not until he needed the scissors that the terrible fact burst upon him. Eppie had run out by herself and, perhaps, had fallen into the Stone Pits. There was one hope—that she had crept into the fields. Silas searched in vain, and then looked with dying hope at the small pond nearby. Here, however, sat Eppie, talking cheerfully to her small boot, which she was using as a bucket.

Here was clearly a case that demanded severe treatment. But Silas, overcome with joy at finding his treasure again, could only snatch Eppie up and cover her with half-sobbing kisses.

It was only when he had carried her home that he remembered the need to punish Eppie. The idea that she might run away gave him resolve.

"Naughty, naughty Eppie," he began. "Naughty to cut with the scissors and run away. Father must put her in the coal-hole." He half expected that Eppie would begin to cry. Instead of that, she looked pleased at the new idea. He put her in the coal-hole, and held the door closed. After a moment, there was the little cry, "Opy, opy!" and Silas let her out again. "Now, Eppie will never be naughty again, else she must go in the coal-hole."

In half an hour, she was clean again, and Silas went back to work, thinking she would be good for the morning and did not need to be held with the linen band. He turned round and was going to place her in her little chair. She peeped out at him with black face and hands again, and said, "Eppie in the coal-hole!"

This total failure shook Silas's faith in punishment. So, Eppie was reared without punishment. The stone hut was made a soft nest for her, lined with patience. She knew nothing of frowns and denials.

In the old days there were angels who came and took people by the hand. And they led them away from the city of destruction. We see no white-winged angels now, yet people are led away from destruction. A hand is put into theirs which leads them gently toward a calm and bright land. And the hand may be a little child's.

There was one person who watched with sharper, though more hidden, interest the growth of Eppie under the weaver's care. Was he very uneasy at his inability to give his daughter her birthright? I cannot say that he was. The child was being taken care of. She would very likely be happy, as people in humble station often were happier, perhaps, than those brought up in luxury.

Godfrey Cass's cheek and eye were brighter than ever now. Dunsey had not come back. People had made up their minds that he was gone "out of the country." Everybody said Mr. Godfrey had taken the right turn. It was pretty clear what would be the end of things. There were not many days in the week when he was not seen riding to the Lammeters' house.

He saw himself with all his happiness centered on his own hearth. And Nancy would smile on him as he played with the children. And that other child—not on the hearth—he would not forget it. He would see that it was well provided for. That was a father's duty.

Chapter 9

It is a bright autumn Sunday, 16 years after Silas Marner had found his new treasure on the hearth. The bells of the old Raveloe church are ringing. Their cheerful sound tells that the morning service is ended. Among the advancing groups of people, there are some whom we shall recognize. This is true in spite of Time, who has laid his hand on them all.

The tall blond man of 40 has not much changed in features from the Godfrey Cass of 26. He is only fuller in flesh, and has only somewhat lost the look of youth. Perhaps the pretty woman, not much younger than he, who is leaning on his arm, is more changed than her husband. The lovely bloom that used to be always on her cheek now comes not as often. Yet there are some who love human faces best for what they tell of human experience. To them, Nancy's beauty has a heightened interest.

Mr. and Mrs. Godfrey Cass have turned around. They look for the tall aged man and plainly dressed woman who are a little behind. Nancy had said that they must wait for "father and Priscilla." Now they all turn into a narrow path leading across the churchyard opposite the Red House. We will not follow them. There are some others in this group whom we should like to see again.

It is impossible to mistake Silas Marner. His large brown eyes seemed to have gathered a longer vision. But in everything else, one sees signs of a body much weakened by the passage of 16 years. The weaver's bent shoulders and white hair give him almost the look of advanced age. In truth, he is not more than 55.

70

But there is the freshest blossom of youth by his side. It is a blond, dimpled girl of 18, who has tried to smooth her curly hair under her bonnet. Eppie cannot help being rather troubled by her hair. For there is no other girl in Raveloe who has hair at all like it.

There is a good-looking fellow in a new suit who walks behind them. She surely knows that there is someone behind her who is thinking about her. And he is gathering courage to come to her side as soon as they are out in the lane.

"I wish we had a little garden, Father, like Mrs. Winthrop's," Eppie said. They moved out into the lane. "Only they say it would take a deal of digging and bringing fresh soil. And you couldn't do that, could you, Father? Anyway, I shouldn't like you to do it. The work would be too hard for you."

"Yes I could do it, child, if you want a bit of a garden," Silas said.

"*I* can dig it for you, Master Marner," said the young man. He was now by Eppie's side.

"Eh, Aaron, my lad, are you there?" Silas said. "I wasn't aware of you. Well, if you could help me with the digging, we might get a garden all the sooner."

"I'll come to the Stone Pits this afternoon," Aaron said. "And we'll settle what land is to be taken in."

"Not if you don't promise me not to work at the hard digging, Father," Eppie said. "You won't work in it till it's all easy. You and me can mark out the beds, and make holes and plant the roots. It will be a deal livelier at the Stone Pits when we've got some flowers. And I'll have a bit of rosemary and thyme, because they're so sweet-smelling. But there's no lavender. It's only in the gentlefolks' garden, I think."

"That's no reason why you shouldn't have some," Aaron said. "For I can bring you slips of anything. I'm forced to cut no end of them when I'm gardening and throw them away. There's a big bed of lavender at the Red House. The missus is very fond of it."

"Well, don't make free for us, or ask anything that is worth much at the Red House," Silas said. "Mr. Cass has been so good to us. He's built us the new end of the cottage, and given us beds and things."

"There's not a garden in the whole parish where there's not endless waste," Aaron said. "But I must go back now. Or else mother will worry."

"Bring her with you this afternoon, Aaron," Eppie said. "I shouldn't like to decide about the garden and not have her know everything from the start," she said. "Should you, Father?"

"Ay, bring her if you can, Aaron," Silas said. "She's sure to have a word to say to help us set things right."

Aaron turned back up to the village. Silas and Eppie went on up the lonely sheltered lane.

After dinner, Eppie glanced up at the clock. "Oh, Father, you want to go into the sunshine to smoke your pipe. But I must clear everything away first. The house must be tidy when godmother comes. I'll make haste. I won't be long."

Now that she was grown up, Silas had often talked to Eppie about his past. He told her how and why he had lived a lonely man until she had been sent to him. It would have been impossible for him to hide from Eppie that she was not his own child. She had long known how her mother had died on the snowy ground. She knew how she had been found on the hearth by her father Silas, who had taken her golden curls for his treasure.

For a long while it did not even occur to Eppie that she must have had a father. The first time it did was when Silas showed Eppie the wedding ring that had

been taken from her mother's finger. It had been carefully kept by Silas in a box. Eppie often opened the
box to look at the ring. But she thought hardly at all
about the father of whom it was the symbol. Besides,
she had a father very close to her. He loved her better
than any real fathers in the village seemed to love
their daughters.

Who her mother was, and how her mother came to
die, were things that often pressed on Eppie's mind.
Her knowledge of Mrs. Winthrop made Eppie feel that
a mother must be very precious. She had often asked
Silas to tell her how her mother looked and how he
had found her against the bush. The bush was still
there. On the afternoon, when Eppie and Silas came
out into the sunshine, it was the first object that
caught Eppie's eyes and thoughts.

"Father, we shall take the bush into the garden,"
Eppie said.

"Ah, child, it wouldn't do to leave out that bush,"
Silas said. "There is nothing prettier, when it's yellow
with flowers. But it's just come into my head. We must
have a fence. Or else the donkeys and things will come
and trample everything down."

"Oh! I'll tell you, Father," Eppie said. "There's lots of
loose stones about. Some of them are not too big. We
might make a wall. You and me could carry the small-
est. And Aaron could carry the rest. I know he would."

"There aren't enough stones to go around," Silas
said.

"Well, if there aren't enough to go all round, they'll
go part of the way. See here, round the big pit, there
are many stones."

She skipped forward to the pit, meaning to lift one
of the stones. But she started back in surprise.

"Oh, Father, come and see how the water's gone

down since yesterday. Why, yesterday the pit was ever so full!"

"Well, to be sure," Silas said coming to her side. "Mr. Godfrey Cass has gone into the draining."

"How odd it will seem to have the old pit dried up," Eppie said, turning away.

"Come, let us sit down on the bank," Silas said.

They sat in silence for a while. Finally, Eppie said gently, "Father, if I were to be married, ought I to be married with my mother's ring?"

"Why, Eppie, have you been thinking about it?" asked Silas, in a low tone.

"Only this last week, father," Eppie said. "Since Aaron talked to me about it. He said he should like to be married. He said he was going on 24 and has a good deal of gardening work now."

"And who is it he's wanting to marry?" said Silas, with a rather sad smile.

"Why, me, Father," Eppie said with laughter. "As if he'd want to marry someone else!"

"And you mean to have him, do you?" Silas said.

"Yes, sometime," Eppie said. "I don't know when. Everybody's married sometime, Aaron says. But I told him that wasn't true. For I said, look at Father. He's never been married."

"No, child," Silas said. "Your father was a lone man till you were sent to him."

"But you'll never be alone again, Father," Eppie said. "That was what Aaron said. 'I could never think of taking you away from Master Marner, Eppie.' He wants us all to live together. He'd be as good as a son to you. That was what he said."

"And should you like that, Eppie?" asked Silas.

"I shouldn't mind it, Father," Eppie said. "I like Aaron to be fond of me and come and see us often. But

I don't want any change. Only Aaron made me cry a bit because he said I didn't care for him. For if I cared for him, I should want us to be married, as he did."

"Eh, my blessed child," Silas said. "You're very young to be married. We'll ask Mrs. Winthrop—we'll ask Aaron's mother what she thinks. If there's a right thing to do, she'll know. But there's this to be thought on, Eppie. Things will change, whether we like it or not. I shall get older and more helpless and be a burden on you. I'd like to think you'd have somebody else besides me—somebody young and strong to take care of you."

"Then, would you like me to be married, Father?" Eppie said, with a little trembling voice.

"I won't be the man to say no," Silas said. "We'll ask your godmother. She'll wish the right thing by you and her son, too."

"There they come, then," Eppie said. "Let us go and meet them."

Chapter 10

Silas and Eppie continued to sit along the bank and talk. At the same time, Priscilla Lammeter was resisting her sister's arguments that she and her father should take tea at the Red House. The family party of four were seated around the table in the parlor. They had their Sunday dessert of fresh nuts, apples, and pears before them.

"Now Father, is there any call for you to go home to tea?" Nancy said. "Can't you just as well stay with us? It's likely to be a beautiful evening."

The old gentleman had been talking with Godfrey. He had not heard the talk between his daughters.

"My dear, you must ask Priscilla," he said. "She manages me and the farm, too."

"Then manage so as you may stay to tea, Priscilla," Nancy said. She put her hand on her sister's arm with affection. "Come now, we'll go round the garden while Father has his nap."

"My dear child, he'll have a beautiful nap in the gig.[1] For I shall drive. And as for staying for tea, I can't hear of it. But there will be time for us to walk while the horse is being readied."

When the sisters began their walk, Priscilla went on. "I'm glad that your husband is making the exchange of land with cousin Osgood and beginning the dairying," she said.

"Ah, Priscilla," Nancy said. "It won't mean much to Godfrey. A dairy is not so much to a man. And it's only what worries him that ever makes me low. I'm

---

1. gig two-wheeled, one-horse carriage

contented with the blessings we have, if he could be contented."

"That's the way of the men always wanting and wanting and never easy with what they've got."

"Oh, don't say so, Priscilla," Nancy said. "Nobody has any occasion to find fault with Godfrey. It's natural he should be disappointed at not having any children. He always counted on making a fuss with them when they were little. There are many other men who would complain more than he does. He's the best of husbands."

"Oh, I know," Priscilla said. "Father will be waiting for me. We must turn now."

The large gig with the steady old gray horse was at the front door. Mr. Lammeter was already on the stone steps talking to Godfrey.

"Bring Nancy to our house before the week is out, Mr. Cass," Priscilla said as she took the reins. She shook them gently and urged the horse forward.

"I shall just take a turn to the fields against the Stone Pits, Nancy," Godfrey said. "I want to look at the draining."

"You'll be in again by teatime, dear?"

"Oh, yes. I shall be back in an hour."

It was Godfrey's custom on a Sunday afternoon to take a walk and think about his farming. Nancy seldom went with him. When Priscilla was not with her on these occasions, she usually sat and read the Bible. And after a while, she would permit her thoughts to wander.

There was one main thread of painful experience in Nancy's married life. Her deepest wound came from the thought that the absence of children from her hearth was something her husband could never accept.

Yet Nancy might have been expected to feel the

absence even more. Wasn't there a drawer filled with the neat work of her hands, not worn or touched, just as she had arranged it 14 years ago? Only the one little dress had been used. It had been used for the burial.

Always, when Nancy thought about it, she tried to see everything as Godfrey saw it. She asked herself the same questions. Had she done everything in her power to lighten Godfrey's loss? Had she really been right in resisting her husband's wish that they adopt a child?

Adoption was not as common in the ideas and habits of that time than in our own. Still, Nancy had her opinion about it. To adopt a child because children of your own had been denied you was to try and choose your lot in spite of God's will. The adopted child, she was convinced, would never turn out well.

"But why should you think the child would turn out ill?" Godfrey said. "She has done as well as a child can do with the weaver. And he adopted her. There isn't such a pretty little girl anywhere in the parish. Or one fitter for the station we could give her. Where can be the likelihood of her being a curse to anybody?"

"Yes, my dear Godfrey," Nancy said. "The child may not turn out ill with the weaver. But then he didn't go to seek her, as we would be doing. It will be wrong. I feel sure it will. Dear Godfrey, don't ask me to do what is wrong. I should never be happy again. I know it's very hard for you. It's easier for me. And it's the will of God."

Godfrey had from the beginning mentioned Eppie as a suitable child for them to adopt. Eppie was then about 12 years old. It had never occurred to Godfrey that Silas would rather part with his life than part with Eppie. Surely the weaver would wish the best for the child. He would be glad that such good fortune should happen to her. She would always be very grateful to him. And he would be well cared for to the end of his life.

"I was right," Nancy said to herself when she recalled all their discussions. "I feel I was right to say no to him, though it hurt me more than anything. But how good Godfrey has been about it! Many men would have been very angry with me for standing against their wishes. Godfrey has never been the man to say an unkind word. It's only what he can't hide. Everything seems so blank to him. And the land— what a difference it would make, when he goes to see after things. If only he had children growing up that he was doing it all for! But I won't murmur. Perhaps another woman who might have given him children would have troubled him in other ways."

Godfrey was always aware of his wife's loving effort. It was impossible to have lived with her for 15 years and not be aware of it. It also seemed impossible that he should ever confess to her the truth about Eppie. She would never recover from the disgust that the story of his earlier marriage would create. And the child, too, he thought, must become an object of disgust. The very sight of her would be painful. He had married Nancy with that secret in his heart. He must keep it there to the last.

Meanwhile, why could he not make up his mind to the absence of children? I suppose it is the way with all men and women who reach middle age not knowing that life never can be completely happy.

As time passed on, under Nancy's refusal to adopt Eppie, correcting his error became more and more difficult. On this Sunday afternoon, it was already four years since they had discussed the subject. Nancy supposed that it was forever buried.

Someone opened the door at the other end of the room. Nancy felt that it was her husband. She turned from the window with gladness in her eyes.

"Dear, I'm so thankful you've come," she said, going toward him. "I began to get...."

She paused abruptly. Godfrey was laying down his hat with trembling hands. He turned toward her with a pale face and a strange glance.

"Sit down, Nancy—there," he said. He pointed to a chair opposite him. "I came back as soon as I could. I wanted to prevent anybody telling you but me. I've had a great shock. But I care most about the shock it will be to you. It's Dunstan—my brother Dunstan, that we lost sight of 16 years ago. We've found him. Found his body—his skeleton.

"The Stone Pits have gone dry suddenly," Godfrey went on. "From the draining, I suppose. And there he lies—has lain for 16 years, wedged between two great stones. There's his watch, and my gold-handled hunting whip, with my name on it. He took it away the day he went hunting with Wildfire. That was the last day he was seen."

Godfrey paused. It was not so easy to say what came next. "Do you think he drowned himself?" Nancy said. She was wondering why Godfrey should be so deeply shaken by what happened all those years ago to an unloved brother.

"No, he fell in," Godfrey said. Then he added, "Dunstan was the man that robbed Silas Marner."

The blood rushed to Nancy's face and neck at this surprise and shame. "Oh, Godfrey!" she said with compassion in her tone.

"There was the money in the pit," he continued. "All the weaver's money. Everything has been gathered up. And they've taken the skeleton to the Rainbow. But I came back to tell you."

He was silent, looking on the ground for two long minutes. Nancy would have said some words of comfort then. But she didn't. She had a sense that Godfrey had something else to tell her.

Then he lifted his eyes to her face. "Everything comes to light, Nancy, sooner or later," he said. "I've lived with a secret on my mind. But I'll keep it from you no longer. I wouldn't have you learn it from somebody else. I wouldn't have you find it out after I'm dead. I'll tell you now.

"Nancy, when I married you, I hid something from you," Godfrey said slowly. "Something I should have told you. That woman Marner found dead in the snow—Eppie's mother. That wretched woman was my wife. Eppie is my child."

He paused, dreading the effect of his confession. Nancy sat quite still. Only her eyes dropped. She was as pale and quiet as a statue.

"I shouldn't have left the child unowned. I shouldn't have kept it from you. But I couldn't bear to give you up, Nancy. I was led away into marrying her. I suffered for it."

Still Nancy was silent, looking down. He almost expected she would get up and say she would go to her father's. How could she have any mercy for faults that must seem so black to her? But at last she lifted up her eyes to his again and spoke. There was no anger in her voice—only deep regret.

"Godfrey, if you had told me this six years ago, we could have done some of our duty to the child. Do you think I'd have refused to take her in, if I'd known she was yours?

"And—Oh, Godfrey," she went on. "If we'd had her from the first, she'd have loved me for her mother. You would have been happier with me. I could have better stood my little baby dying. Our life might have been more like we used to think it would be."

The tears fell. And Nancy ceased to speak.

"But you wouldn't have married me then, Nancy, if I'd told you," said Godfrey, as if trying to prove to himself he had done the right thing. "You may think you would now, but you wouldn't then. With your pride and your father's, you'd have hated having anything to do with me."

"I can't say what I should have done about that, Godfrey. I should never have married anyone else. But I wasn't worth doing wrong for. Nothing is in this world. Nothing is as good as it seems beforehand. Not even our marrying was, you see." There was a faint sad smile on Nancy's face as she said the last words.

"I'm a worse man than you thought I was, Nancy," Godfrey said. "Can you forgive me ever?"

"The wrong to me is little, Godfrey. You've made it up to me. You've been good to me for 15 years. It's another you did the wrong to. And I doubt it can ever be made up for."

"But we can take Eppie, now," Godfrey said. "I won't mind the world knowing at last. I'll be plain and open for the rest of my life."

"It will be different coming to us, now she's grown up," Nancy said. "But it's your duty to acknowledge her and provide for her. And I'll do my part by her. And pray to God Almighty to make her love me."

"Then we'll go together to Silas Marner's this very night. We'll go as soon as everything is quiet at the Stone Pits."

Chapter 11

Between eight and nine o'clock that evening, Eppie and Silas were seated alone in the cottage. Silas sat in his armchair and looked at Eppie. She had drawn her own chair toward his knees and leaned forward. She held both his hands while she looked up at him. On the table near them, lit by a candle, lay the recovered gold. It was arranged in orderly heaps, as Silas used to arrange it. He had been telling her how he used to count it every night. And he told her how empty his soul had been until she was sent to him.

"You didn't know then, Eppie, when you were such a little one. You didn't know what your old father Silas felt for you."

"But I know now, Father," Eppie said. "If it hadn't been for you, there would have been nobody to love me."

"Eh, my precious child, the blessing was mine. If you hadn't been sent to save me, I should have gone to the grave in my misery. The money was taken from me in time. And you see it's been kept till it was wanted for you. It's wonderful—our life is wonderful."

Silas sat for a few moments, looking at the money. "The money takes no hold of me now," he said. "I wonder if it ever could again. I doubt it might, if I lost you, Eppie. I might come to think I was lost again."

At that moment there was a knocking at the door. Eppie rose and opened it. When she saw Mr. and Mrs. Godfrey Cass, she made a little curtsy and held the door wide for them to enter.

"We're disturbing you very late, my dear," Nancy said, taking Eppie's hand.

Eppie placed chairs for Mr. and Mrs. Cass. Then she went to stand beside Silas opposite them.

"Well, Marner, it's a great comfort to me to see you with your money again," Godfrey said. "It was one of my family that did you wrong. And I feel bound to make up to you for it in every way. Whatever I can do for you will be nothing but paying a debt, even if I looked no further than the robbery. But there are other things I'm in debt to you for, Marner."

Godfrey checked himself. It had been agreed between him and his wife that the subject of his father-hood should be approached very carefully. If possible, it should be revealed in the future.

"Sir, I have a great deal to thank you for already," Silas said. "As for the robbery, you couldn't help it."

"You may look at it that way, Marner, but I never can," Godfrey said. "I hope you'll let me act according to my own feeling of what's just. I know you've been a hard-working man all your life."

"Yes, sir," Silas said.

"Ah," Godfrey said. "But you're getting rather past such close work, Marner. It's time you had some rest. You look a good deal pulled down, though you're not an old man, are you?"

"Fifty-five, as near as I can say, sir."

"You've done a good part by Eppie for 16 years. It would be a great comfort to you to see her well provided for, wouldn't it? You'd like to see her taken care of by those who can leave her well off and make a lady of her."

"I don't take your meaning, sir," Silas said.

"Well, my meaning is this, Marner," Godfrey said. "Mrs. Cass and I, you know, have no children. We have nobody to benefit by our good home and everything else we have. And we should like to have somebody in the place of a daughter to us. We should like to have Eppie and treat her in every way as our own child. It would be a great comfort to you in your old age, I hope, to see her fortune made in that way. And it's right that you should have every reward for that. Eppie, I'm sure, will always love you and be grateful to you. She'd come and see you very often. And we should all be on the lookout to do everything we could to make you comfortable."

Silas was silent for some moments when Mr. Cass had ended. Eppie's heart was swelling at the sense that her father was in distress. Then Silas said faintly, "Eppie, my child, speak. I won't stand in your way. Thank Mr. and Mrs. Cass."

"Thank you, ma'am—thank you, sir," Eppie said. "But I can't leave my father. And I don't want to be a lady—thank you all the same." (Here, Eppie made another curtsy.) "I couldn't give up the folks I've been used to." Silas, with a muffled sob, put up his hand to grasp hers.

Godfrey was irritated. He spoke again, this time with a feeling of excitement mixed with anger.

"But I've a claim on you, Eppie, the strongest of all claims. It's my duty, Marner, to own Eppie as my child and provide for her. She is my own child. Her mother was my wife. I have a natural claim on her that must stand before every other."

Eppie had given a violent start, and turned quite pale. "Then, sir, why didn't you say so 16 years ago?" Silas said with a touch of bitterness. "Why didn't you claim her before I'd come to love her, instead of coming to take her from me now? You might as well take the heart out of my body. God gave her to me because you turned your back upon her. He looks upon her as mine. You've no right to her! When a man turns a blessing from his door, it falls to them who takes it in."

"I know that, Marner. I was wrong. I've repented my conduct in that matter."

"I am glad to hear it, sir," Marner said. "But that doesn't change what's been going on for 16 years. Your coming now and saying 'I'm her father' doesn't change the feelings inside us. It's me she's been calling her father ever since she could say the word."

"But I think you might look at the thing more reasonably, Marner," Godfrey said. "It isn't as if she were to be taken quite away from you, so that you'd never see her again. She'll come to see you very often. She'll feel just the same toward you."

"Just the same?" Marner said, more bitterly than ever. "Just the same? That's idle talk. You'd cut us in two."

"I should have thought your affection for Eppie would have made you rejoice in what was for her good," Godfrey said. "Even if it did call upon you to give up something. She might marry some low working-man. And then whatever I might do for her, I couldn't make her well-off. You're putting yourself in the way of her welfare. I'm sorry to hurt you after what you've done. But I feel now it's my duty to insist on taking care of my own daughter."

It would be difficult to say whether it was Silas or Eppie that was more deeply stirred by this last speech. "I'll say no more," Silas said. "Let it be as you will. Speak to the child. I'll hinder nothing."

"Eppie, my dear," Godfrey began. "It will always be our wish that you should show your love and gratitude to one who's been a father to you so many years. We shall want to help you make him comfortable in every way. But we hope you'll come to love us as well. I haven't been what a father should have been to you all

these years. But I wish to do everything in my power for you for the rest of my life. And you'll have the best of mothers in my wife. That will be a blessing you haven't known since you were old enough to know it."

"My dear, you'll be a treasure to me," said Nancy in her gentle voice.

Eppie did not come forward and curtsy as she had done before. She held Silas's hand in hers and grasped it firmly. She spoke with colder decision than before. "Thank you ma'am—thank you, sir, for your offers," she said. "They're very great and far above my wish. For I should have no delight in life anymore if I were forced to go away from my father. He's taken care of me and loved me from the first. I'll stay with him as long as he lives. And nobody shall ever come between him and me."

"But you must make sure, Eppie," Silas said, in a low voice. "You must make sure you won't ever be sorry. Because you've made your choice to stay among poor folks, with poor clothes and things. You might have had everything of the best."

"I can never be sorry, Father," Eppie said.

Nancy thought there was a word that might come better from her lips that from her husband's.

"What you say is natural, my child," she said. "But there's a duty you owe to your lawful father. When your father opens his home to you, I think it's right you shouldn't turn your back on it."

"I can't feel as if I've got but one father," Eppie said, while the tears gathered. "I can't think of another home. I wasn't brought up a lady. I like the working folks and their houses and their ways. And I've promised to marry a working-man, who will live with Father and help me take care of him."

Godfrey looked up at Nancy. He had a flushed face

and tears in his eyes. "Let us go," he said quietly.

"We won't talk of this any longer now," Nancy said, rising. "We're your well-wishers, my dear. And yours too, Marner. We shall come and see you again. It's getting late."

In this way she covered her husband's quick departure. For Godfrey had gone straight to the door, unable to say more.

Nancy and Godfrey walked home under the starlight in silence. When they arrived at the house, they entered the oaken parlor. Godfrey put out his hand and Nancy placed hers within it. He drew her toward him and said, "That's ended!"

"Yes, I'm afraid we must give up the hope of having her for a daughter. It wouldn't be right to force her to come to us against her will. We can't change her bringing up and what's come of it."

"No," Godfrey said. "There are debts we can't pay like money debts, by paying extra for the years that have slipped by. Marner was right about a man's turning away a blessing from his door. It falls to somebody else. I wanted to pass for childless once, Nancy. I shall pass for childless now against my wish."

"You won't make it known, then, about Eppie's being your daughter? If not, I shall be thankful for Father and Priscilla never to be troubled."

"No, where would be the good to anybody? Only harm. I think I shall put it in my will." He paused for a moment. "I've an idea it's Aaron Winthrop whom Eppie is engaged to. I remember seeing him with her and Marner leaving church."

"Well, he's very hard-working," Nancy said.

Godfrey was thoughtful again. Then he looked up at Nancy sadly. "She's a very pretty, nice girl, isn't she,

Nancy?"

"Yes, dear, and with just your hair and eyes."

"I think she took a dislike to me at the thought of my being her father. I could see a change in her manner after that."

"She couldn't bear to think of not looking on Marner as her father," Nancy said.

"She thinks I did wrong by her mother as well as by her," Godfrey said. "She thinks me worse than I am. But she must think it. She can never know all. It's part of my punishment, Nancy, for my daughter to dislike me. I should never have got into that trouble if I'd been true to you. I'd no right to expect anything but evil to come of that marriage.

"And I got you, Nancy, in spite of it all," Godfrey went on. "And yet I've been grumbling and uneasy because I hadn't something else—children. As if I deserved it."

"My only trouble would be gone if you accepted the lot that's been given us," Nancy said.

"Well, perhaps it isn't too late to mend a bit there. Though it *is* too late to mend some things."

Chapter 12

The next morning, Silas and Eppie were seated at the breakfast table. "Eppie, there's a thing I've had on my mind to do for two years," Silas said. "And now that the money has been brought back to us, we can do it. We'll leave the house, and we'll make a little bundle of things and set out."

"Where to go, Father?" said Eppie, in much surprise.

"To my old country," Silas said. "To the town where I was born—Lantern Yard. I want to see Mr. Paston, the minister. Something may have come out to make them know I was innocent of the robbery. And I should like to talk to the minister about the religion of this countryside."

So four days later, Silas and Eppie were making their way through the streets of a great manufacturing town. Silas was bewildered by the changes that 30 years had brought to his native place. He stopped several people to ask them the name of this town. He wanted to be sure he was not making a mistake about it.

"Ask for Lantern Yard, Father," Eppie said. "Ask this gentleman standing at the shop door."

"He won't know anything about it," Silas said. "Gentlefolks didn't ever go up to the Yard. But maybe somebody can tell me which is the way to Prison Street, where the jail is. I know the way out of that as if I'd seen it yesterday."

With some difficulty, after many questions, they reached Prison Street. "Ah, there's the jail," Silas said, drawing a long breath. "I'm not afraid now. The third turn on the left from the jail doors, that's the way we must go."

They came to a narrow alley. "Here it is," he said, "And then we must go to the left again and forward for a bit, up Shoe Lane."

They finally reached Shoe Lane. "Dear heart!" Silas said. "Why there are people coming out of the Yard as if they'd been to chapel at this time of day!"

Suddenly, he stood still with a look of amazement. They were before an opening in front of a large factory. Men and women were streaming out of it for their midday meal.

"Father, what's the matter?" Eppie said, clasping his arm.

"It's gone, child," he said at last, very upset. "Lantern Yard's gone. They've made this new opening—and see that big factory! It's all gone—chapel and all."

"Come into that little brush shop and sit down, Father," Eppie said. "Perhaps the people can tell you all about it."

But neither from the brushmaker, nor from anyone else, could Silas learn anything of the old Lantern Yard friends, or of Mr. Paston, the minister.

"The old place is all swept away," Silas said to Dolly Winthrop on the night of his return. "I shall never know whether they got at the truth of the robbery. And I'll never know whether Mr. Paston could have given me any light about the drawing of the lots. It's dark to me, Mrs. Winthrop. I'm sure it will be dark to the last."

"Well, yes, Master Marner," Dolly said. "It's the will of Them above that many things should be dark to us. But there are some things I've never felt in the dark about. And they're mostly what comes in the day's work. You were hard done by that once, Master Marner. And it seems that you'll never know the rights of it. But that doesn't prevent there being rights, Master Marner. Even though it's dark to you and me."

"No, that doesn't," Silas said. "Since the time that the child has come to me, and that I've come to love her as myself, I've had light enough to trust by. And now she says she'll never leave me. I think I shall trust till I die."

The sunshine fell more warmly on the lilacs the morning that Eppie was married. As she walked across the churchyard and down the village, she seemed to be dressed in pure white. Her dress was a very light one, and it had been provided by Mrs. Godfrey Cass. Her hair looked like the dash of gold on a lily. One hand was on her husband's arm. With the other, she clasped the hand of her father Silas.

"You won't be giving me away, Father," she said before they went to church. "You'll only be taking Aaron to be a son to you."

Dolly Winthrop walked behind with her husband. And there ended the little bridal procession.

There were many eyes to look at it. Miss Priscilla Lammeter was glad that she and her father had arrived at the Red House just in time to see this pretty sight. They had come to keep Nancy company today. Mr. Cass had had to go away to Lytherley. That seemed to be a pity. For otherwise he might have gone, as Mr. Crackenthorp and Mr. Osgood certainly would, to look at the wedding feast that Mr. Cass had ordered at the Rainbow. Naturally, he had a great interest in the weaver who had been wronged by one of his own family.

In the open yard before the Rainbow, the party of guests were already assembled. It was still nearly an hour before the feast time. It allowed the guests much time to talk of Silas Marner's strange history. They concluded that he had brought a blessing on himself by acting like a father to a lone, motherless child. And there was general agreement with Mr. Snell's view. When a man deserved his good luck, Mr. Snell said, it was the part of his neighbors to wish him joy.

As the bridal party approached, a hearty cheer was raised in the Rainbow. The party continued on to the Stone Pits. Eppie had a larger garden there than she had ever expected. There had been other changes, at the expense of Mr. Cass, to suit Silas's larger family. He and Eppie had declared that they would rather stay at the Stone Pits than go to any new home. The garden was fenced with stones on two sides. In the front there was an open fence, through which the flowers shone with answering gladness as the four united people came within sight of them.

"Oh, Father," said Eppie, "what a pretty home ours is! I think nobody could be happier than we are."

REVIEWING YOUR READING

CHAPTER 1

FINDING THE MAIN IDEA

1. Silas Marner has to leave his native town because
    (A) he can't find work   (B) his girlfriend moves away   (C) he is falsely accused of a crime   (D) he has to go to a warmer climate.

REMEMBERING DETAILS

2. Silas's closest friend in Lantern Yard is
    (A) Sally Oates   (B) William Dane   (C) Mrs. Osgood   (D) Jem Rodney.

DRAWING CONCLUSIONS

3. People in Raveloe think that Silas may be possessed by the devil because
    (A) he is a weaver   (B) he is from Lantern Yard   (C) he lives alone   (D) he sometimes has fits.

USING YOUR REASON

4. William Dane probably steals the money and frames Silas because
    (A) he wants to take Sarah away from Silas   (B) he hates the deacon of the church   (C) he hates weavers   (D) he believes the church had stolen his money.

THINKING IT OVER

5. Why do you think Silas Marner refuses to become part of the community of Raveloe when he moves there? Explain.

CHAPTER 2

FINDING THE MAIN IDEA

1. Godfrey Cass is afraid that his brother Dunstan will reveal that
    (A) Godfrey is secretly married   (B) Godfrey hates their father
    (C) Godfrey has killed his horse   (D) Godfrey plans to leave home.

96

REMEMBERING DETAILS

2. To get money, Dunstan suggests that Godfrey
   (A) rob a bank   (B) borrow it from their father   (C) sell his horse
   (D) ask his wife.

DRAWING CONCLUSIONS

3. Godfrey is afraid that if his father learns of his secret he will
   (A) make him get a job   (B) disown him and throw him out
   (C) move to another town   (D) tell Nancy Lammeter.

USING YOUR REASON

4. Dunstan first visits Silas Marner with the intention of
   (A) robbing him   (B) asking Silas to teach him how to be a weaver
   (C) borrowing some money   (D) asking Silas if he can stay
   overnight.

THINKING IT OVER

6. Why do you think Dunstan Cass steals Silas Marner's gold? Do
   you think he really believes Silas is dead? Or do you think he just
   figures he can steal it and never be caught? Explain.

CHAPTER 3

FINDING THE MAIN IDEA

1. This chapter is mostly about
(A) the escape of Dunstan Cass   (B) Silas Marner's reaction to the
   theft of his gold   (C) the appearance of a ghost at the Rainbow Inn
   (D) an argument between Mr. Dowlas and Mr. Macey.

REMEMBERING DETAILS

2. When he arrives at the Rainbow Inn, Silas first blames the theft on
   (A) Mr. Snell   (B) Dunstan Cass   (C) Jem Rodney   (D) Mr. Macey.

DRAWING CONCLUSIONS

3. The landlord says that Jem Rodney couldn't have stolen Silas's
   gold because
   (A) Jem Rodney couldn't be in two places at the same time
   (B) Jem Rodney didn't know Silas had any gold   (C) Silas is Jem
   Rodney's best friend   (D) Jem Rodney is afraid of Silas because of
   Silas's trances.

98

USING YOUR REASON

4. Mr. Dowlas, the farrier, is convinced that the robbery can be explained in terms of human behavior because

   (A) he is the one who stole the money (B) he knows that Dunstan Cass is the thief (C) he doesn't believe in ghosts (D) he just wants to argue with the others at the Rainbow.

THINKING IT OVER

5. What does the theft of the gold represent to Silas? As you form your answer, think of the importance that Silas places on the gold before it is taken from him.

CHAPTER 4

FINDING THE MAIN IDEA

1. This chapter is mostly concerned with Godfrey's decision to

   (A) tell his father about the money he gave Dunstan (B) find out what happened to Dunstan (C) marry Nancy Lammeter (D) ask Bryce for the money for Wildfire.

REMEMBERING DETAILS

2. Squire Cass offers to speak for Godfrey in the matter of Godfrey's

   (A) marrying Nancy Lammeter (B) getting the money back from Dunstan (C) buying a horse to replace Wildfire (D) finding a new place to live.

DRAWING CONCLUSIONS

3. Squire Cass probably feels that Nancy's father wouldn't object to Nancy marrying Godfrey because

   (A) the Squire knows that Nancy's father likes Godfrey very much (B) the Squire is the wealthiest man in Raveloe (C) Nancy's father and the Squire are best friends (D) Nancy's father has always said Godfrey should marry Nancy.

THINKING IT OVER

4. At the end of the chapter, Godfrey is uneasy because he is "tangled up in more lies and deceit." What extra trouble is he in? Explain.

CHAPTER 5

FINDING THE MAIN IDEA

1. The theft of Silas's gold causes most people in Raveloe to
(A) dislike Silas even more (B) think he is stupid (C) feel sorry
for him (D) ignore him.

REMEMBERING DETAILS

2. The person who comes to visit Silas just before Christmas is
(A) Justice Malam (B) Nancy Lammeter (C) Dunstan Cass
(D) Dolly Winthrop.

DRAWING CONCLUSIONS

3. The townspeople of Raveloe don't connect Dunstan's disappearance
with the theft of Silas's gold because
(A) Dunstan is known as an honest fellow (B) Dunstan has made
similar disappearances before (C) Dunstan isn't a peddler
(D) everyone knows that Dunstan likes Silas too much to steal
from him.

USING YOUR REASON

4. Godfrey's constant companion, Anxiety, shows that Godfrey
(A) has a guilty conscience about the life he is leading (B) is
enjoying his life as a liar (C) talks to himself too much
(D) doesn't worry enough about things.

THINKING IT OVER

5. Why do you think the people in Raveloe are less frightened by and
more sympathetic to Silas after his gold has been stolen? Explain.

CHAPTER 6

FINDING THE MAIN IDEA

1. At the great New Year's Eve party, Godfrey Cass
(A) proves he is a great dancer (B) tries to show Nancy Lammeter
that he still cares greatly for her (C) argues with his father
(D) proposes to Nancy Lammeter.

REMEMBERING DETAILS

2. Nancy and Godfrey have to leave the dance floor because

(A) they have an argument   (B) Nancy's dress is damaged
(C) Nancy's sister is taken ill   (D) Godfrey steps on her feet.

DRAWING CONCLUSIONS

3. Nancy Lammeter acts coldly toward Godfrey at the dance because

    (A) she is tired of his treatment of her   (B) he is a bad dancer
    (C) she wants him to pay attention to her sister   (D) her father
    doesn't like Godfrey.

USING YOUR REASON

4. Godfrey is probably pleased that Nancy shows a flash of anger
    because

    (A) he wants to get her mad   (B) it shows she cares enough about
    him to become angry   (C) he wants to marry her sister (D) he is
    very stupid.

THINKING IT OVER

6. Why do you think Nancy doesn't tell Godfrey to leave her alone
    when he asks her if she wants him to go? Explain.

CHAPTER 7

FINDING THE MAIN IDEA

1. This chapter is mostly concerned with Silas Marner

    (A) going to the New Year's Eve party   (B) discovering a little girl
    in his cottage   (C) giving shelter to Godfrey's wife   (D) getting
    his gold back.

REMEMBERING DETAILS

2. The woman named Molly Farren is

    (A) Godfrey's wife   (B) Silas Marner's sister   (C) Silas Marner's
    wife   (D) Dunstan Cass's wife.

DRAWING CONCLUSIONS

3. If Silas had not been in a trance when the little girl entered the
    cottage, he

    (A) would have refused to let her come in   (B) invited her to have
    dinner with him   (C) discovered the girl's mother lying in the
    snow much sooner   (D) accompanied the mother to the New
    Year's Eve party.

USING YOUR REASON

4. Godfrey doesn't plan to tell Nancy that Molly had been his wife because
   (A) he feels Nancy won't have anything more to do with him
   (B) Nancy will feel sorry for him   (C) he will have to leave Raveloe   (D) Nancy will want to pay for Molly's funeral.

THINKING IT OVER

5. When Godfrey looks at his dead wife's face, the author writes that he remembers every line as he told the full story 16 years later. To whom and why do you think Godfrey might tell this story? Explain.

CHAPTER 8

FINDING THE MAIN IDEA

1. Silas's decision to keep and raise Eppie as his daughter causes
   (A) his neighbors to hate him   (B) Dolly Winthrop' jealousy
   (C) little Eppie to cry   (D) his neighbors to think more kindly of him.

REMEMBERING DETAILS

2. Silas decides to name the little girl after
   (A) his dead wife   (B) his mother and dead sister   (C) Dolly Winthrop's mother   (D) Nancy Lammeter's mother.

DRAWING CONCLUSIONS

3. Silas doesn't want anyone to know that he had been in a trance when Eppie came into his cottage because
   (A) he thinks everyone will laugh at him   (B) the parish might take Eppie away from him   (C) Eppie will think he was strange
   (D) someone might think he is trying to steal the girl from her mother.

USING YOUR REASON

4. Silas probably decides to have Eppie christened in the Raveloe church because
   (A) he suddenly becomes religious   (B) Eppie asks him to do it
   (C) the rector asks him to do it   (D) he wants Eppie to be accepted by the community.

THINKING IT OVER

5. At the end of the chapter, the author writes that Godfrey feels he will see that Eppie is provided for while not admitting she was his real daughter. Why is he choosing this action?

CHAPTER 9

FINDING THE MAIN IDEA

1. It's clear from this chapter that for the past 16 years, Silas and Eppie have

    (A) been very happy together (B) disliked each other (C) lived separately (D) visited Godfrey and Nancy Cass very often.

REMEMBERING DETAILS

2. On the way home from church, Eppie asks Silas if they can have

    (A) some new furniture (B) a new house (C) a garden (D) some house pets.

DRAWING CONCLUSIONS

3. Eppie is curious about her dead mother, but never asks about her real father because

    (A) she has always thought of Silas as her father (B) it is too painful for her to think about (C) she knows her real father is Godfrey (D) she doesn't understand what a father is.

USING YOUR REASON

4. Eppie wants to continue living with Silas even after she gets married probably because

    (A) Silas owes her money (B) Silas asks her to (C) Aaron wants to (D) she has grown so attached to Silas over the years.

THINKING IT OVER

5. How do you think Silas feels about the idea of Eppie marrying Aaron? Use evidence from the chapter to support what you say.

CHAPTER 10

FINDING THE MAIN IDEA

1. This chapter is mostly concerned with

    (A) Nancy's father and sister paying a visit (B) Godfrey visiting

the Stone Pits   (C) Nancy's depression over losing her baby
(D) Godfrey's confession about his first marriage and his being
Eppie's father.

REMEMBERING DETAILS

2. People in Raveloe learn that Dunstan had stolen Silas Marner's
gold when
(A) Dunstan finally confesses   (B) Dunstan's skeleton is
discovered with the bags of gold in the drained Stone Pits   (C) it is
revealed in Squire Cass's last letter   (D) Nancy's father tells
everyone about it.

DRAWING CONCLUSIONS

3. For 16 years, Godfrey never confesses to Nancy that Eppie is his
real daughter because
(A) he is almost certain that Nancy will leave him   (B) Eppie asks
him not to tell   (C) he forgets Eppie is his daughter   (D) he
doesn't want to embarrass Nancy's father and sister.

USING YOUR REASON

4. When Nancy says that Godfrey has wronged someone else more
than her, she is talking about
(A) Silas   (B) Dolly Winthrop   (C) Eppie   (D) Priscilla.

THINKING IT OVER

5. Why do you think Godfrey decides to confess to Nancy about his
past marriage and his real daughter when the only thing he has to
tell her about is Dunstan's death and the robbery?

CHAPTER 11

FINDING THE MAIN IDEA

1. When Eppie learns that Godfrey Cass is her real father, she
(A) refuses to leave Silas and live with Godfrey and Nancy
(B) becomes furious with Godfrey   (C) runs to Nancy and calls
her "Mommy"   (D) leaves Silas forever.

REMEMBERING DETAILS

2. At first, Godfrey tells Silas he wants Eppie to come and live with
him because

(A) he and Nancy have no children of their own (B) he has always loved Eppie (C) he promised his father he'd adopt Eppie (D) Eppie is his real daughter.

DRAWING CONCLUSIONS

3. When Silas tells Eppie that the gold "takes no hold of me now," he means that

(A) he now hates gold (B) he plans to give the gold away (C) Eppie is now more important to him than the gold (D) he wishes the gold had never been found.

USING YOUR REASON

4. Eppie probably refuses Godfrey's offer to come and live with him because

(A) she doesn't like Nancy (B) she loves Silas and feels loyal to him (C) she wants to inherit Silas's gold (D) she wants to learn how to be a weaver.

THINKING IT OVER

6. Do you think Eppie made the right decision? Should she have taken advantage of the opportunity for a much better life? Or was she right to have stayed with Silas? Explain.

CHAPTER 12

FINDING THE MAIN IDEA

1. When Silas returns to Lantern Yard, he discovers that

(A) everybody remembers him well (B) he is still being accused of stealing the money (C) not much has changed since he'd been away (D) the whole town has disappeared.

REMEMBERING DETAILS

2. The chapel and everything else at Lantern Yard have been replaced by a

(A) shoe store (B) new church (C) large farm (D) large factory.

DRAWING CONCLUSIONS

3. Godfrey Cass sponsors the wedding feast for Eppie and Aaron, but then leaves town because

(A) he hates Aaron (B) he can't bear seeing his real daughter get

married without getting to show he is her father   (C) Nancy asks
him to leave   (D) Eppie asks him to leave.

USING YOUR REASON

4. When Silas says he has come to love Eppie and that he will trust
    till he dies, he means that
    (A) he can trust Eppie with his gold   (B) Eppie's love has restored
    his faith in people   (C) he can trust Eppie to marry Aaron
    (D) Dolly is right to trust people.

THINKING IT OVER

5. In her book, what do you think George Eliot is saying about the
    value people place on things as opposed to the value of love?
    Explain.